3

"David Jeremiah has been an incredible inspiration and encouragement to me over the years. His books continue to challenge me in my walk with God. In this book, *Prayer: the Great Adventure,* he has once again challenged me to take a good hard look at my prayer life and ask the question, "Why do I pray?"

Unfortunately, for many of us, our need for God doesn't become desperate until tragedy strikes. This has been true in my own life. Through cancer I became desperate, not only because I needed God's strength for the journey but because I was also desperate to tell Him how much I needed Him. Over the past few years I have lost that attitude toward prayer because life has become comfortable once again. I needed to be smacked up side the head, to be reminded that without Him I am nothing. Thank you, David, for reminding me that my prayers must be out of desperation no matter what the circumstance."

DAVE DRAVECKY
COLORADO SPRINGS, CO

"If you're tired of books written with the 'saint' in mind—books which say good and true things about prayer but aren't very helpful—this is your book. Biblical and practical, this book could send you on an…well, an adventure. David Jeremiah has paid his dues…and now he shares with us the reality he has discovered. Don't miss this one!"

STEVE BROWN
KEY LIFE NETWORK
MAITLAND, FL

'o subject could be more timely in our day than David Jeremiah's
yer: the Great Adventure. There is a beautiful honesty in his handling of
promises, pitfalls, and power potential connected to the simple act of
ing. Read it and be inspired to call on God in a new and deeper way."

PASTOR JIM CYMBALA
THE BROOKLYN TABERNACLE
BROOKLYN, NY

"My life resonates with David Jeremiah's feeling that sometimes he is praying to his computer. In our see-it, grab-it, sinkhole society, prayer as a habitual pattern seems like a misfit, but the writer's stepping stones to making Jesus' agenda our own provide a clear guide to mastering this life-changing discipline."

HOWARD G. HENDRICKS
DISTINGUISHED PROFESSOR
CHAIRMAN, CENTER FOR CHRISTIAN LEADERSHIP
DALLAS THEOLOGICAL SEMINARY

"Bravo! Dr. Jeremiah gives us a powerful and sincere message concerning prayer. His personal testimony demonstrates firsthand the example that Christ set forth for us in the Gospels. Read it and discover the keys to unlock your own adventure to glorious prayer."

BILL GAITHER
ALEXANDRIA, IN

PRAYER
—THE GREAT—
ADVENTURE

DAVID JEREMIAH

MULTNOMAH PUBLISHERS, INC.

SISTERS, OREGON

PRAYER
THE GREAT ADVENTURE
published by Multnomah Publishers, Inc.

© 1997 by David Jeremiah

Published in association with the literary agency of Yates and Yates,
505 S. Main, Suite 100, Orange, CA 92668.

International Standard Book Number: 1-57673-131-6

Cover photograph by Rodney Oman Bradley

Printed in the United States of America

Most Scripture quotations are from:
New American Standard Bible (NASB) © 1960, 1977 by the Lockman Foundation, used by permission.

Also quoted:
The Holy Bible, New International Version (NIV) © 1973, 1984
by International Bible Society, used by permission of Zondervan Publishing House
The Holy Bible: authorized King James Version (KJV).
The Bible: The New King James Version © 1984 by Thomas Nelson, Inc.

For information:
Multnomah Publishers, Inc. • Post Office Box 1720 • Sisters, Oregon 97759

Library of Congress Cataloging–in–Publication Data
Jeremiah, David.
    Prayer:the great adventure/by David Jeremiah.
        p.cm.
    Includes bibliographical references.   ISBN 1-57673-131-6 (alk. paper)
    1. Prayer--Christianity. I. title
BV215.J47   1997
248.3'2--dc21   97-20802
                                                                              CIP

        97 98 99 00 01 02 03 — 10 9 8 7 6 5 4 3 2 1

To the Watchmen on the Wall
of the Shadow Mountain Community Church
who stand watch day and night through intercessory prayer.

"Praying always with all prayer and supplication in the Spirit,
being watchful to this end with all perseverance and
supplication for all the saints."

EPHESIANS 6:18

CONTENTS

INTRODUCTION: THE ADVENTURE AWAITS 11

PART ONE: THE ADVENTURE BEGINS

1 THE GREAT ADVENTURE OF PRAYER 19

2 TOO BUSY NOT TO PRAY 35

3 IT PAYS TO PRAY 49

PART TWO: DIGGING FOR GOLD

4 A ROADMAP FOR PRAYER 69

5 PRAISE: APPROACHING A HOLY FATHER 83

6 PRIORITIES: ALIGNING OUR WILL WITH GOD'S . . . 101

7 PROVISION: ASKING FOR WHAT WE NEED 119

8 PERSONAL RELATIONSHIPS:

   LIVING IN THE JOY OF FORGIVENESS 135

9 PROTECTION: SEEKING SAFETY FROM HARM 153

10 ENDING WHERE WE BEGAN 171

PART THREE: SEE HOW IT GLITTERS

11 THE GREATEST PRAYER EVER OFFERED 191

12 SECRETS OF THE DIRECTED LIFE 207

13 A PERSONAL MAP TO BURIED TREASURE 223

    RECOMMENDED READING 243

    SOURCE NOTES 245

    INDEXES 253

ACKNOWLEDGMENTS

The New Testament uses many intense words to describe the discipline of prayer—*agonize, wrestle, labor, groan*—just to mention a few. Similar words could be employed to describe this attempt to write about prayer. At times, it has been an agonizing experience. I am grateful to those who have jumped into the midst of the battle and provided strength and encouragement.

Sealy Yates has been a constant encouragement and has kept me focused on the importance of this project.

Steve Halliday has liberally invested his gifts as writer and editor.

Helen Barnhart has worked diligently to type and retype manuscripts.

Glenda Parker has watched over my schedule so I could have blocks of time to study.

My son, **David Michael,** has picked up a huge part of the load at Turning Point so that my mind could be freed of administrative details.

Paul Joiner has illustrated many of the concepts in this book with his dramatic productions each Sunday. Some of his pictures have been translated into words.

My wife, **Donna,** continues to be my greatest human inspiration for all that I do.

INTRODUCTION

In his classic work *With Christ in the School of Prayer,* Andrew Murray pointedly writes, "Moses gave neither command nor regulation with regard to prayer: even the prophets say little directly of the duty of prayer. It is Christ who teaches to pray."[1]

Jesus is our tutor and example in all things, and nowhere is that more clear than in our prayer lives. It is no exaggeration to say that prayer undergirded and preceded and empowered everything that our Lord did while He walked on this earth. He frequently spoke about prayer and even more frequently taught by example. It is a telling fact that "Jesus never taught His disciples how to preach, only how to pray. He did not speak much of what was needed to preach well, but much of praying well. To know how to speak to God is more important than knowing how to speak to man. Not power with men, but power with God is the first thing. Jesus loves to teach us how to pray."[2]

How glad I am that He is still in the business of teaching His children how to pray! Although I have prayed since childhood, my praying habits have changed a great deal in the past few years. There is something different and new about my praying these days—and it is not hard at all to identify the reason for the change. A couple of years ago I was diagnosed with cancer and very quickly prayer took on new meaning for me. I discovered a dimension to prayer that I had never known before. Jesus enrolled me in His intensive course on prayer and I became an eager learner.

And what lesson struck home with most force? I discovered something that had been true all along, even though I had not thought much about it. *I discovered I was helpless without God!* That was the beginning of the adventure for me.

I learned how to pray out of desperation. For most of us, this is how the adventure usually begins. When we finally get serious about prayer, the trigger is usually desperation, not duty. Andrew Bonar wrote in 1853, "God likes to see His people shut up to this. That there is no hope but in prayer. Herein lies the Church's power against the world."[3]

At least initially, serious prayer is almost always driven by necessity. We don't pray because we *ought*, we pray because we are without any other recourse. I think God likes to see His people coming to Him in desperation and casting themselves upon His mercy! Jim Cymbala said something in his new book *Fresh Wind, Fresh Fire*, that I can identify with: "Prayer cannot truly be taught by principles and seminars and symposiums. It has to be born out of a whole environment of felt need. If I say, 'I *ought* to pray,' I will soon run out of motivation and quit; the flesh is too strong. I have to be *driven* to pray."[4] Jack Taylor agrees with this conviction. He writes, "Our infirmities are the trumpets which call us to prayer. No miracle was performed in the Bible that did not begin in a problem.... The greater the problem, the greater the solution."[5]

Could it be that one reason we have great problems is that God wants to show us great solutions? He longs to show us the riches of His grace and the poverty of our own resources. Prayer is uniquely designed to demonstrate both truths.

Yet at the same time, we must remember that prayer is not a natural activity. It has been well said that prayer is stupid when viewed in the purely human realm. I remember the day I realized why it was so hard for me to pray. I wrote this down in my Bible: "Prayer is my Declaration of Dependence." As one author has written:

> Prayer is the essential activity of waiting for God: acknowledging our helplessness and his power, calling upon him for help, seeking his counsel. So it is evident why prayer is so often commanded by God, since his purpose in the world is to be exalted for his mercy. Prayer is the antidote for the disease of self-confidence.[6]

For a go-getter, type A, driven person (like me), prayer is the most difficult thing of all because it flies in the face of our frantic efforts to prove that we are self-sufficient, independent, and strong. We somehow forget that "the difference between Uncle Sam and Jesus Christ is that Uncle Sam won't enlist you in his service unless you are healthy, and Jesus won't enlist you unless you are sick. 'Those who are well have no need of a physician, but those who are sick; I came not to call the righteous, but sinners' (Mark 2:17). Christianity is fundamentally convalescence ('Pray without ceasing' = Keep buzzing the nurse)."[7]

My bout with cancer taught me a lot about "buzzing the nurse"! The fears and desperation which forced me to my knees taught me to cry out to God as never before. And do you know what? He heard! He answered! He delivered me from all my fears! And He desires to do the same for you.

WISDOM FOR THE JOURNEY

During those long months of battling my illness, I not only prayed with greater urgency, but I also devoured the words of other saints who before me had begun their own adventures in prayer. I was encouraged and strengthened and buoyed as I read their powerful insights. In my personal journal I copied the quotations that especially helped me, wise statements such as the following:

> To [Jesus] prayer is everything; it's a duty as well as a privilege, a right as well as a responsibility. We tend to use prayer as a last resort, but Jesus wants it to be our first line of defense. We pray when there's nothing else we can do, but Jesus wants us to pray before we do anything at all.[8]

Untutored, we tend to think that prayer is what good people do when they are doing their best. It is not. Inexperienced, we suppose that there must be an "insider" language that must be acquired before God takes us seriously in our prayer. There is not. Prayer is elemental, not advanced, language. It is the means by which our language becomes honest, true, and personal in response to God. It is the means by which we get everything in our lives out in the open before God.[9]

Though in its beginnings prayer is so simple that the feeblest child can pray, yet it is at the same time the highest and holiest work to which man can rise.[10]

There is a direct correlation between not knowing Jesus well and not asking much from Him. A failure in our prayer life is generally a failure to know Jesus.... A prayerless Christian is like a bus driver trying alone to push his bus out of a rut because he doesn't know Clark Kent is on board.... A prayerless Christian is like having your room wallpapered with Sak's Fifth Avenue gift certificates but always shopping at Ragstock because you can't read.[11]

Prayer does not fit us for the greater works; prayer is the greater work.[12]

As long as we look on prayer chiefly as the means of maintaining our own Christian life, we shall not know fully what it is meant to be. But when we learn to regard it as the highest part of the work entrusted to us, the root and strength of all other work, we shall see that there is nothing that we so need to study and practice as the art of praying aright.[13]

What a person wants is somewhere to rest his mind and heart, and the only place to rest is in God, and the only way to come to God is by prayer. Much of our prayer has nothing in it; it is the talk of a child to his Father when he has come up against things or is hurt.[14]

There are two kinds of prayer: personal and intercessory.... Christ has opened the school of prayer specially to train intercessors for the great work of bringing down, by their faith, and prayer, the blessings of His work and love on the world around.[15]

True prayer, that takes hold of God's strength, that availeth much, to which the gates of heaven are really opened wide—who would not cry, "Oh for someone to teach me thus to pray"?[16]

It's amazing how many coincidences occur when one begins to pray.[17]

This book is a direct result of my experiences over the past few years. I did not write it as an "expert" on prayer; I am nothing but a fellow learner. Jesus has taught me much about prayer through His Word and through some hard lessons of life, and my hope is that I might be able to encourage you in some small measure by relating what I have learned.

WHAT YOU WILL FIND

I have divided the book into three sections. Part One, "The Adventure Begins," considers several of our Lord's general teachings on prayer and answers several key questions, such as:

- How can I find time to pray when I'm so busy?
- What's the best way to overcome discouragement in prayer?
- Why do I have to ask?

Part Two is titled "Digging for Gold" and explores the breathtaking riches found in what we often call "The Lord's Prayer." We discover here that this model prayer can inform and energize our own praying like nothing else.

Part Three, "See How It Glitters," zooms in on what has rightly been called "the greatest prayer in history," our Lord's High Priestly Prayer of John 17. Here we see prayer at its most powerful and most sublime. After we have gathered several of this prayer's gems, we end the book with a chapter on journaling, a discipline that has immeasurably enriched my personal prayer life.

Throughout these pages I have reproduced snippets from my personal journal, both to illustrate the benefits of journaling and to recall the faithfulness and love of a God who delights in answering the prayers of His people. As I culled several hundred pages of journal notes in preparing to write this book, I was forcefully reminded once more of the boundless mercy and grace of our heavenly Father. What a God we serve!

It is my profound hope that this book might serve as a springboard to launch even a few of God's people into greater depths of prayer. I am praying that many who read it will catch the same spirit of excitement that I feel about this subject! I am convinced that until we get serious about prayer, we cannot know the half of our Lord's desire for our lives. I can shout a wholehearted "amen!" to the writer who said,

> God wants to meet your deepest needs. He wants you to see, know, taste, and experience Him in ways that shake you to your core. He longs for you far more than you long for Him. He stands ready to reveal himself, enfold you in love, speak to you with power, and touch you with grace. He has waited for you— for this moment. Are you ready?[18]

I would ask the same question: Are you ready? The Lord invites you to come to Him in prayer. The great adventure awaits!

Part One

THE ADVENTURE BEGINS

Chapter One

THE GREAT ADVENTURE OF PRAYER

S o many of the books I've read on prayer seem to be little more than guilt-ridden tirades on why we don't pray and why we should pray more. Let me say at the outset of our journey together that I have no intention of adding to such a depressing collection. What I want to do in this book, if I can, is to help us catch a glimpse *of what we might be missing* by not making prayer a vital part of our lives. I have found that prayer is the most wonderful gift in God's great bag of blessings. It is the great adventure of the Christian faith.

No matter who we are or what our life circumstances may be, prayer can become for us a thrilling, daily adventure. So many of us are needlessly living at a level far beneath that which God wants for us. He has a storehouse full of rich provisions, just waiting to be distributed to all those who will simply ask Him to open His hand. So often it is true that we have not because we ask not.

If I accomplish anything at all in this first chapter, I hope I will light a fuse in your heart that will explode into an insatiable craving for God's best in your life. I invite you to explore the possibility that, just maybe, you could be missing out on something wonderful and indescribable—

yet something easily attainable and which God has designed to bless you beyond all imagining.

A TREASURE MAP TO UNTOLD RICHES

To begin our great adventure, let's consider a great teaching on prayer uttered by the Lord Jesus. It is God's treasure map to find hidden, untold riches. Here is the map:

> Ask, and it shall be given to you; seek, and you shall find; knock, and it shall be opened to you. For everyone who asks receives, and he who seeks finds, and to him who knocks it shall be opened. Or what man is there among you, when his son shall ask him for a loaf [of bread], will give him a stone? Or if he shall ask for a fish, he will not give him a snake, will he? If you then, being evil, know how to give good gifts to your children, how much more shall your Father who is in heaven give what is good to those who ask Him! (Matthew 7:7–11)

As I read that passage, I can't sniff even a particle of guilt anywhere in it. Can you? Jesus does not want to goad us into praying as much as He desires to entice us into it!

It's almost as if He says to us, "Come, partake of My banquet. It's free! Do you see the freshly-baked bread, piled high on one table? It is for you. Can you smell the delicious aroma of the roasted main course, the sweet fragrance of the pastries and pies and cakes, the wholesome fragrance of newly-picked vegetables and fruits? It's all yours. I have provided all you need. I have enough for everyone and there is no need to fear that I will run out of food. I am inviting you to My feast. Your place is reserved at My table. All I require is that you ask My Father to give you what you need. That's it! That is the only thing lacking."

THE IMPERATIVES OF PRAYER

This great passage on prayer was given to us by the Lord in His Sermon on the Mount. It represents the second time in that sermon that He speaks about prayer. Already His disciples had come to Him and asked, "Lord, teach us to pray." At that time He taught them what is commonly called the Lord's Prayer (we will savor that prayer at length in chapters 4–10). Now Jesus returns to the subject again. Interestingly, this is the only subject Jesus addressed twice in the Sermon on the Mount. Clearly, the issue of prayer was vitally important to Him.

ASK, DON'T BEG

Jesus tells us, "Ask and it will be given to you; seek and you will find; knock and it will be opened unto you." So that we don't miss His point, our Lord uses the word "ask" five times in this passage. "Ask," says the Lord. He doesn't say beg. He merely says, ask.

This can only mean that God is not waiting for us to bang down His heavenly door and implore Him, though there is the issue of persistence in prayer (see chapter 3). The real issue is this: We have not because we ask not.

In the weeks I spent preparing to write this book, a number of people came to me and told me about their problems, asking for counsel on how to deal with them. I have to admit, I've never been so straightforward before: "Have you asked God about it?" More often than not, the reply was, "Well…no, I guess I haven't."

Let me tell you, asking God is a good place to start! Why would anyone come to David Jeremiah before they would approach the Creator of the universe? I don't have much to give; God has whole worlds in His back pocket.

The Bible says we don't have because we don't ask. So if we don't have it, and we need it, maybe we ought to try asking for it. Jesus didn't tell us five times to "ask" in this passage because He had nothing better to say. He *wants* us to ask. The question is, will we?

A USEFUL ACROSTIC

Notice what happens if you take the three imperatives in this verse—ask, seek, and knock—and put them underneath each other:

A s k

S e e k

K n o c k

Even the three words themselves cry out to us to ask. Ask! Seek! Knock! What does Jesus want us to do when it comes time to pray? *Just ask*.

Don't you love it when you hear new believers pray? They haven't learned "Christianese" yet. Nobody has taught them all the Thees, Thous and Thys. They simply talk to God. "God, here I am. It's me. It's Jim. Yeah, I need this, Lord." That's the simplicity Jesus asks of us. We're to come to God as children, as dependents. And (may I say it again?) we're to ASK.

Have you ever noticed how children ask? Boy, do they ask—freely and often! One story tells of a little boy who was misbehaving one night when his father was trying to get him into bed. The boy's mother had gone to a meeting and his father was taking care of things at home. Long after the little boy had been tucked in for the night, he was doing the classic drink of water routine: "Dad? I need a drink of water." His father came upstairs and gave him a drink of water, and of course a short time later the boy had to go to the bathroom. This happened several times. Finally the exasperated dad reached the limit of his patience and said, "No more. Young man, you get into bed and you stay there."

A few minutes later, however, this father heard the pitter-patter of little feet upstairs. He bolted to the foot of the stairs, this time angry that his reading had been interrupted. He yelled up to his misbehaving son,

"Look, I'm telling you for the last time! You get in bed and you *stay* in bed! If you get out of bed one more time, you're in trouble. I'll be coming up there and you'll get a whipping!"

For a moment it was very quiet. Then a little voice drifted down: "Daddy, when you come up here to give me a whipping, could you bring me a glass of water?"

That's how children are. They never quit. It doesn't matter how many times you say no, they keep coming back. They keep asking. They ask and ask and ask.

I think that's what Jesus is talking about here. He wants us to come to Him and…ask.

WORDS OF ESCALATING INTENSITY

The three words in this passage are all imperatives (or commands) and each word is a little more intense than the word preceding it. First we ask, then if we *ask* and don't hear the answer, we are to *seek* out the person. What does it mean to seek? You search for the person. Why should we seek out God? I think it's because, if we're not careful, we can sometimes get caught up in the gift and forget about the Giver. God wants a personal connection with us. We need to get back to the Giver and we do that by "seeking." If after we've asked we don't think we're hearing the answer, maybe we need to go back and seek the One of whom we are making our request.

After we ask and we seek, an even more intense activity might be required. Jesus tells us to *knock*. When I hear this word I get a mental picture of a person asking a friend for something, but not getting an answer. So he circles his friend's house, searching for him. If he doesn't see him outside, he goes up to the door and starts knocking: "Would you please come?"

Ask, seek, knock. These are all imperatives. They're commands. Jesus is not saying to us, "If you feel like it, ask. If you're into this, seek.

If it's the way you feel today, knock." No. He's saying, "Here's how you pray. This is My command to you. Ask. If you want Me to act on your behalf, My requirement is that you ask." Whatever we need, we must ask for it.

PRAYING LIKE A CHILD

One of my professors in seminary, Dr. Howard Hendricks, told us how a highly intelligent lecturer came for a visit in his home. After the man had settled in and everyone sat down to eat, the Hendricks family had a little time of family worship. When it came time to pray, the children, in typical childlike fashion, thanked Jesus for the tricycle and the sandbox and the fence. Later this very sophisticated theologian began to chide Dr. Hendricks: "You don't mean to tell me that you're a professor in a theological seminary and you teach your children to pray for things like that?"

"I certainly do," replied Dr. Hendricks, who then asked a question of his own: "Do you ever pray about your Ford?" Dr. Hendricks knew the man did, because the vehicle was riding mostly on faith and frayed fabric.

"Oh, of course I pray for my Ford," said the lecturer, "but that's different."

"Oh, really?" said Dr. Hendricks. "What makes you think your Ford is more important to God than my boy's tricycle?" Then he pressed him further. "You're on the road a lot. Do you ever pray for protection?"

"Brother Hendricks, I never go anywhere but that I pray for the Lord's journeying mercies."

"Well, safety is essentially what my boy is praying about when he thanks Jesus for the fence. That fence keeps those big dogs on the other side. Is it any different for him to pray for safety than it is for you?"

The lecturer, of course, had no answer. For prayer is not only about high-powered theological concerns, but about tricycles and fences and childlike requests made in simple faith. Jesus tells us to ask, to seek, to knock, in the simplicity of childlike prayer. And He promises that our prayers will be heard.

THE INFLUENCE OF PRAYER

In verse 8 Jesus tells us, "For everyone who asks receives, and he who seeks finds, and to him who knocks it will be opened." Two things here are of special note.

Prayer Is Comprehensive

One word is particularly crucial in this verse: *Everyone*. When it comes to hearing His children, God's ears are not at all selective. He doesn't listen only to some special somebodies like pastors or prayer warriors or Christian workers or writers. He hears *everyone*! That word fairly jumps off the page. "For *everyone* who asks..."

Now obviously, Jesus is talking about people who know Him. He's not talking to pagans. The "everyone" of this passage is the everyone of the whole sermon—it was directed to those who knew God. Are you a Christian? If so, then you're an "everyone" and this promise is for you. Some of us don't pray because we think, *Well, that's for those folks. You know, Pastor Jeremiah, he prays, and I'm sure that some of the folks who are deacons, they pray. But I'm just an average Joe. I mean, let other people pray.*

O, don't let that attitude take up residence in your mind! You have no idea how quickly it will crowd out all the blessings God wants to give you. Jesus could not have been more clear. This is a comprehensive promise. *Everyone*. That's you, mister. That's you ma'am. That's you, young man, young lady. Everyone. You can get in on this no matter who you are, as long as you know the Lord.

Prayer Is Certain

Jesus not only invites everyone to pray, He says that "Everyone who asks *receives*" and "Everyone who seeks *finds*" and "to him who knocks, *it will be opened*." This is an ironclad promise. Andrew Murray wrote about this text,

Ask and you shall receive; everyone that asks, receives. This is the fixed eternal law of the kingdom: if you ask and receive not, it must be because there is something amiss or wanting in the prayer. Hold on; let the Word and Spirit teach you to pray aright, but do not let go the confidence He seeks to waken: Everyone who asks receives…. Let every learner in the school of Christ therefore take the Master's word in all simplicity…. Let us beware of weakening the Word with our human wisdom.[1]

If you are a child of God, know with certainty that your heavenly Father wants to answer your prayer!

For a lot of years, I floated around with the idea that prayer was something I was "supposed" to do because the Bible says I am supposed to do it—and that's true. But since I've been getting a few answers to prayer, I've become increasingly excited that these promises from God are legitimate, true, and certain. God means to answer your prayer and mine. It is certain.

Let me encourage you that if you have never had the opportunity to see God answer your prayers, if you've never prayed for anything specifically and seen God answer, you can begin right now on this great adventure. Don't wait any longer to begin. Why miss out on the greatest blessing of your life?

I know that some Christians don't spend much time praying because they don't believe they will ever see any answers. Perhaps they prayed in the past for something of vital interest to them and didn't receive the answer they had hoped for. So they stopped praying altogether. J. Oswald Sanders pointed to this problem when he wrote, "It is easy to become a fatalist in reference to prayer. It is easier to regard unanswered prayer as the will of God than to… reason out the causes of the defeat."[2]

And what could be some of those reasons for "defeat"? Oswald Chambers had at least one suggestion when he wrote, "Our Lord in His teaching regarding prayer never once referred to unanswered prayer; He said God always answers prayer. If our prayers are in the name of Jesus, that is, in accordance with His nature, the answers will not be in accordance with our nature, but with His. We are apt to forget this, and to say without thinking that God does not always answer prayer. He does every time, and when we are in close communion with Him, we realize that we have not been misled."[3]

But what if you believe you are praying in God's will for something He delights in, and yet there is no answer? James Montgomery Boice suggests, "If you are praying for something and God is not answering your request with a 'Yes,' ask what you can accomplish in the meantime and give yourself to that. It does not mean that God may not give you what you are asking for eventually, but in the meantime you will be doing good work."[4]

I think that is excellent advice. But the best advice of all is this: *Just keep praying!* When I started keeping a prayer journal a couple of years ago, I began to write down my requests. Toward the end of last year and the early part of this year, I've been rereading those journals to harvest them and recall what God has done in my life in response to my prayers. It's been thrilling to see that, back here I prayed for this (and I almost forgot that I prayed for it) and then out here God answered it. Sometimes the answer was so specific it was almost frightening. To think that God, the Ruler of the universe, would do that for me for no other reason than that I asked. It staggers me! Answered prayer is the most wonderful of all His gifts. Nothing is better. I can only repeat that if you're not praying, you're missing out on the great adventure.

I agree with Andrew Murray who wrote, "If there is one thing I think the Church needs to learn, it is that God means prayer to have an answer, and that it hath not entered into the heart of man to conceive what God will do for His child who gives himself to believe that his prayer will be heard."[5]

THE ILLUSTRATION OF PRAYER

In order for us to really grab hold of this exciting invitation, the Lord Jesus gives us an illustration in verses 9 and 10. He says, "What man is there among you, when his son shall ask him for a loaf, will give him a stone? Or if he shall ask for a fish, he will not give him a snake, will he?"

STONES, BREAD, FISH AND SERPENTS

This story has a Palestinian context. Do you recall the Gospel account of Christ's temptation in the wilderness? Satan said to Him, "Why don't you make these stones into bread?" Do you know why he asked Him to do that? Why not ask that the stones be made into lamb chops or veal or green beans? The most likely reason is that the stones in Palestine often *look* like little loaves of bread. The stones are of that size and would remind anyone of bread. Satan crafted his temptation to be as obvious and inviting as possible.

Now, back to our passage. Jesus asks, what father among us would give a stone to his son if he should ask for a loaf of bread? Who would reach down, hand his boy a rock from the ground, and say, "Here, son, sink your teeth into this"? Do you know anyone who would do that? I don't.

Lord, how wonderful to contemplate this thought—that I pray to My Father! I know how I love to help my children—how I delight in meeting their needs, how much joy it brings to me to show them my love through responding to their requests. And now I am reminded that God is my Father and that if I take the best fathering that I have ever done and multiply it exponentially, God is beyond all of that in His desire to meet the needs that I have as His child. What a wonderful thought! How can I pray differently because this has been so powerfully thrust upon my heart today! Lord, this year help me to understand even more that You are my Father, and that You want to hear and answer my prayers as I would my own children!

And how about the second image Jesus uses? Commercial fishermen in ancient Palestine used nets, and as the nets were drawn together, often the men would find water snakes mixed in with their catch of fish. Jesus probably had that in mind when He asked what kind of father would hand his son a snake when he had asked for a fish. You just can't picture it. "Dad, could I have a fish from your catch?" "Sure, son—enjoy this lovely serpent here."

Jesus said, "Hear me now. Listen closely. If you're nowhere as good as God—in fact, you're evil by comparison—and yet you would never think of doing such a thing to your son, how could you ever dream that God, who is good, would treat you like that?" I'm sure that no father reading this book would treat his son or daughter so horribly. Neither would any mother. Most of us want to do the best that we can for our kids. If they ask us for something, and it's reasonable, and we think it's good for them, we'll grant their request.

Jesus is counting on just such a reaction. He says that if you earthly fathers act like that—and your hearts are evil compared to the purity and love of God—then how can you imagine that your heavenly Father would want to do anything less? The illustration is carefully designed to convince us that God longs to answer our prayers.

GOD WANTS TO ANSWER OUR PRAYERS

Where did we get the idea that prayer is breaking down God's reluctance? Why do we so often think that prayer is nothing but bashing in the door of God's unwillingness? The Bible doesn't teach that. The Bible says that God is anxious to answer our prayers, that He's *eager* to do so, that He really wants to grant our requests. If we ask God for something that's good and God sees that it's good for us, He will give it to us. Sometimes our problem is that we ask for a snake and God wants to give us a fish. We beg for a stone but God knows we need bread. God always answers prayer, and although sometimes He may not give us the answer we particularly want, He always answers godly prayer.

Bill Hybels has a little formula in his book, *Too Busy Not to Pray*. He writes, "If the request is wrong, God says, 'No.' If the timing is wrong, God says, 'Slow.' If you are wrong, God says, 'Grow.' And if the request is right, the timing is right, and you are right, God says, 'Go.'"[6]

One caution here. I don't want to give the impression that prayer is some sort of carte blanche thing. If you're living like the devil, don't suppose that you can go to God and ask and He will become your heavenly Bellhop and give you whatever you want. That's not going to happen.

But even when we ask amiss, prayer often brings God's will into sharp focus for us. Frequently in the process of prayer, God has first changed *me* so He could answer my prayer! Sometimes my prayer has been misconceived. On occasion I've prayed for something, thinking I knew all of the issues, when in fact I did not. I wasn't even close! But as I've continued to pray, God has helped me to see that my whole perspective was skewed. He has tweaked my prayers and massaged them and put them back. Then He has answered, "OK, David, I can handle that one for you. That's the prayer I want you to pray." And I have received my request.

> *I think that it is an awesome thing to think about the fact that every time we pray we are somehow, some way changed! That should, in itself, draw us to prayer if we desire to be like God! Oh, Lord, I feel like such an infant when it comes to this holy discipline. I praise You for Your patience with me. I do believe that You are in control of the circumstances that have drawn me back to You in a deeper way. I know that I need You, and I know that I am a child in my relationship to You. You are my Father!*

Did you know God has a drawer for you? It has your name on it. Do you know what it's stuffed with? It's full of good things. And God's just waiting for you to ask Him to give you those things.

What is it that you need more than anything else?

Name it.

Now…may I ask a pointed question? Have you asked God for it? Have you really asked Him? God says He is going to answer your prayers. So if His Book is true and He longs to give you good things, then why don't you ask?

THREE APPLICATIONS

This encouraging passage suggests three powerful applications for us. Let's briefly consider all three.

1. *Pray personally*

This text is loaded with personal pronouns. "Let *him* ask." Do you know what I've discovered in talking to some folks? They think that prayer is almost exclusively a corporate activity. If they need prayer, they call the church and everybody prays for them. That's a good thing to do, but corporate prayer is only as good as individual prayer. Churches don't pray; people pray. Families don't pray; individuals pray. Nations don't pray; citizens pray. Prayer is personal. Before I would encourage anyone to join some corporate prayer ministry, I would encourage them to get fired up about their own personal prayer ministry. Why not get personally involved in prayer? It's an out-of-this-world adventure.

2. *Pray particularly*

Jesus wants us to pray for specific things. The illustrations He uses in this text are bread and fish. Why use these particular illustrations? They represent the common, ordinary needs of life. And they are particular. When we pray, we're to pray particularly. It's not necessarily bad to pray, "God, bless all the missionaries in the world" or "Bless all the preachers" or "Please bless my church." I thank God for those prayers—but how much better it would be to get more specific!

Why not pray, "Bless the Sunday School teachers," and then call them by name? Why not ask God to "Bless the missionaries," and then call them by name and mention one or two special needs in their life? Ask God for what you want, specifically. And may I offer one more suggestion? Never pray for anything in such a general way that when your request gets answered, you won't know it. When you pray, pray so specifically that when the answer comes, you'll respond, "Wow! He did it!"

3. *Pray persistently*

We'll talk more about this in chapter 3, but for right now I want to lay a little groundwork. In the Greek language of the New Testament, there are two basic kinds of imperatives. One is called an aorist imperative. An aorist imperative is used to describe an action that takes place once and for all. For instance, suppose you're in a car and giving directions to the driver. At a particular intersection you say, "Stop at that light." Stop is an imperative, but in that context it is an aorist imperative, a once-for-all action. But if you were to say to the driver, "Don't forget to stop at every light," that's a present imperative with continuous action.

Do you know what kind of imperatives Jesus uses in this passage? All three of His commands—ask, seek, knock—are present imperatives. They could be translated this way: "*Keep on* asking, *keep on* seeking, *keep on* knocking."

Don't ever stop asking, don't ever stop seeking, don't ever stop knocking. Just keep at it. Keep bringing your prayers to God. If you think your request is legitimate, keep asking, keep seeking, keep knocking. God wants to teach us through persistent praying to wait on Him and to watch. While we're praying and waiting for God to answer our prayers, do you know what He's doing? He's working on us, conforming us more and more to the image of Christ. And when we're ready, the answer will surely come.

PERSONAL LESSONS ON PRAYER

In the past few years God has taught me more than I can express, through personal, particular, persistent prayer. He's taught me that He can find a Christian oncologist in a hospital in Minnesota where I've never been before, and have him show up right at the time when I need him. He's taught me that He can locate me forty minutes away from the one man who knows more about my disease than any man in the world, and then make it possible for me to be his patient.

> On my desk and in my mail was a large package from someone back east. The outside of the envelope said, "A get-well present for David Jeremiah." When I opened the package, I found a transcript of the series of messages we were planning to run this summer on Turning Point. This lady had transcribed all twelve tapes and had edited them in a beautiful fashion. We were wondering how in the world we were going to get those transcripts done with all that is going on here. As we read through these transcripts, we discovered that they were perfect for our study guides and took incredible pressure off of all of us. What a great present!

He's taught me that I can send my son to a secular university far away, and within two weeks of his arrival discover that the athletic director is a believer, as is the president of the university and his wife (both of whom just happen to listen to Turning Point on the radio).

He's taught me so many personal things about prayer. I'm so glad I didn't wait until it was too late to start asking!

I don't know what your needs are, but I want to tell you something: *We have not because we ask not.* When you're done with this chapter, put this book down, figure out what it is that you really need, and *ask God for it.* Keep good notes. Learn what He wants you to learn. And you will never, ever be sorry. I know that the anonymous author of the following piece wasn't sorry. It's obvious to me that he or she has traveled far in this great adventure of prayer. Enjoy with me the following travelogue this writer left behind for us to ponder:

POWER OF PRAYER

I got up early one morning and rushed into the day;
I had so much to accomplish that I didn't have time to pray.

Problems just tumbled about me, and heavier came each task.
"Why doesn't God help me?" I wondered. He answered, "You didn't ask."

I wanted to see joy and beauty, but the day toiled on, gray and bleak;
I wondered why God didn't show me. He said, "But you didn't seek."

I tried to come into God's presence; I used all my keys at the lock.
God gently and lovingly chided, "My child, you didn't knock."

I woke up early this morning, and paused before entering the day;
I had so much to accomplish that I had to take time to pray.

Chapter Two

TOO BUSY
NOT TO PRAY

P rayer does not come naturally to any of us. In our more honest moments, we all admit it's a struggle to pray as we'd like. And yet there is no avoiding the fact that Scripture insists God has hard-wired the universe in such a way that He works primarily through prayer. No doubt He could have chosen some other method, but He has chosen to do most of His work through prayer. In some ways, He has made Himself subservient to the prayers of His people. And certainly He has conditioned a good portion of His blessing upon our willingness to pray.

So why is it that our prayer lives so often fall short of our prayer desires? If prayer really is a great adventure, then why don't we strike out on spiritual safaris more often? I would hazard a guess that the number one reason is the busyness of our lives. We are *so* busy. There is so much going on; from morning till night it's a rat race. It's a dog-eat-dog world out there, and after eighteen hour days, we lay our tired frames in bed and try to steal as much sleep as we can in the few hours allotted to us. Then, long before dawn breaks (but not before the last possible moment), we get out of bed, grab a quick breakfast, shower, shave, and scurry off to work, hoping we're not late.

And then the thought hits us: *Oh, I really did mean to pray. But somehow I didn't get around to it.*

THE BUSIEST DAY IN JESUS' LIFE

Believe it or not, the One who taught us to pray had a life remarkably similar to our own. Jesus was an incredibly busy man. The Gospels record only fifty-two days of His life, but what a whirlwind of activity is chronicled in those few hundred hours! If you wrote down the events of each day on fifty-two sheets of paper, I doubt if you would have enough room on each page to report even the major incidents that took place. As Donald Whitney wrote,

> Jesus was a busy Man. Read Mark's Gospel and notice how often the word immediately describes the transition from one event in Jesus' life to the next. We read of Him sometimes ministering all day and until after dark, then getting up before dawn to pray and travel to the next ministry venue. The Gospels tell of occasional nights when He never slept at all. They tell us He got tired, so tired that He could sleep in an open, storm-tossed ship. Crowds of people pressed upon Him almost daily. Everyone wanted time with Him and clamored for His attention. None of us knows "job-related stress" like the kind He continually experienced. If Jesus' life, as well as that of Paul, were measured against the "balanced life" envisioned by many Christians today, they would be considered workaholics who sinfully neglected their bodies.[1]

The busiest day of our Lord is recorded in the first chapter of Mark's Gospel. This day was crowded with miracles to perform, lessons to teach, people to heal, disputes to settle. It was a day totally dedicated to reaching out to people and ministering to their deep needs. How draining that kind of intensive ministry can be! It's hard to understand the strain on both mind and body if you've never endured a day of full-bore, non-stop ministry. To keep yourself open to people all day, to serve them and minister to them and help them and teach them and listen to them for hours on end without a break—nothing I know of will suck the life and energy out of a person like intense ministry. And yet that's exactly the kind of day Jesus had in Mark 1.

How can we begin to grasp what that day cost Him? He didn't just preach several sermons and go home to a nice, filling dinner. One after another, people came to him for healing, for understanding, for a gentle touch. Minute after minute, hour after hour, from the rising of the sun until the pale glow of sunset, Jesus worked. People with problems flocked to Him. A son was ill. A daughter was crippled. A neighbor was tormented by a demon. Two friends were arguing over some point of doctrine. And one by one, need after need, Jesus ministered to them all.

Who among us wouldn't be ready to collapse after a day like that? But still Jesus was not done. Mark tells us, "And when evening had come, after the sun had set, they began bringing to Him all who were ill and those who were demon-possessed. And the whole city had gathered at the door" (Mark 1:32–33).

Talk about busy! When was the last time a whole city gathered at our door? Compared to this, what do we know about "busy"?

Eventually, of course, even Jesus needed to rest. But not long after He finally pillowed His head after the busiest recorded day of His life (there's no telling how late it was), we read, "And in the early morning, while it was still dark, He arose and went out and departed to a lonely place, and was praying there" (Mark 1:35).

The morning after is always the hardest, isn't it? You're exhausted. You have nothing left to give. Your bed seems like heaven. That's the morning that you say, "Well, I guess I'll just skip it today."

But not Jesus. The morning after the busiest day of His life was the morning He chose to get up early and pray.

BUT WE'RE JUST ORDINARY FOLKS

"Oh, but that's Jesus," someone will say. "He's the Son of God; I'm just an ordinary person. I could no more pray on a morning like that than I could heal the population of a whole city. Jesus could do it, but I can't."

We might like to follow the Master's example, but we think it's impossible. We can't get all the strings tied; life just won't wrap up the way we want it to. For us, survival is the biggest success story we dare hope for. We are ordinary people, not the Son of God, and we feel "too tired" a lot. We'd like to pray more; we understand that Jesus took time out to pray after the most exhausting day of His life. But that's *Jesus*, we think; we're just plain old people.

And yet the very thing that keeps us from praying is the very reason why we need to pray. Andrew Murray wrote, "It is to prayer that God has given the right to take hold of Him and His strength. It is on prayer that the promises wait for their fulfillment, the kingdom for its coming, the glory of God for its full revelation."[2] Prayer is the means God has chosen to work through us.

THE UNQUESTIONED COMMAND TO PRAY

We all know we are commanded to pray. The Bible is packed from start to finish with encouragements and urgings and commands to pray. The first prayer named as such is found in Genesis 20, where Abraham is instructed by God to pray that the life of Abimelech would be spared. The last recorded prayer in the Bible is found in Revelation 22:20, where John prays, "Come, Lord Jesus." In between those two prayers are scores of instructions for God's people to pray. For example:

- In 1 Samuel 12:23 the prophet Samuel says to the people of Israel, "Far be it from me that I should sin against the LORD by ceasing to pray for you."

- Psalm 32:6, itself a prayer, says, "Let everyone who is godly pray to you while you may be found" (NIV).
- In Isaiah 56:7 the Lord reminds us, "My house will be called a house of prayer for all the peoples." Jesus quoted this verse when He violently cleansed the temple of greedy money changers and other illicit economic activity.
- Colossians 4:2 commands us to "continue in earnest prayer" (NKJV). The word *continue* is the term from which we get our word *strength*. We are instructed to be strong in prayer, to give strength or energy to our praying. This reminds us that prayer is work. It is not an idle pastime, an optional exercise reserved for more "spiritual" believers. Prayer is the hard-work business of the church of Jesus Christ.

Author John Piper compares prayer to a wartime walkie-talkie designed for accomplishing a divine mission. And then he asks this penetrating question: "Could it be that many of our problems with prayer and much of our weakness in prayer come from the fact that we are not all on active duty, and yet we still try to use the transmitter? We have taken a wartime walkie-talkie and tried to turn it into a civilian intercom to call the servants for another cushion in the den."[3] As Piper says, "Life is war."

Colossians 4:12 tells about Epaphras, one of Paul's friends. I love what it says about him: Epaphras "is always wrestling in prayer" (NIV) for the Colossian believers. The intensity and all-out exertion of his prayer life could only be captured in a word taken from athletic competition. He *wrestled* in prayer with God, like Jacob did one night long before (see Genesis 32:22–32). In a similar way, Colossians 2:1 says Paul had a "great conflict" (NKJV) for the people in his prayer ministry.

I wanted to learn more about those words translated "wrestle" and "conflict" (which come from the same root word in Greek), so I tracked down their appearances in the New Testament. You'd be surprised where they're used. For instance, the root word which describes a man agonizing in prayer is also used of a man working until he's exhausted (Colossians 1:29). It's the word used of an athlete competing for a coveted prize (1 Corinthians 9:25). It's the word used of a soldier who battles for his life (1 Timothy 6:12) or of a man struggling to rescue a friend (John 18:36).

I wonder...do those word pictures describe our prayer life? Does it have the sheer *intensity* of an athletic contest? The all-out *agony* of rescuing a friend from drowning? The total *exertion* of an exhausting work day? If so, great! The great adventure of prayer often requires buckets of sweat.

The kind of prayer that will change our lives, our churches, and our world is all business. Prayer that transforms is prayer that gets down to work. It's not an idle word said before mealtime or an exhausted phrase offered before we lay our head on the pillow at night. Those kinds of prayers are good as far as they go, but the problem is, they don't go very far. They don't have much stamina. They can't get a lot of work done. The kind of prayer that changes hearts and transforms neighborhoods and rebuilds communities and revives nations is intense, fervent, and all business. It's that kind of dedicated ministry through which the real work of God gets done. As pastor Bill Hybels has written, "When we work, we work; but when we pray, God works."[4]

DOES GOD DO ANYTHING WITHOUT PRAYER?

I scoured the New Testament some time ago, looking for things God does in ministry that are not prompted by prayer. Do you know what I found?

Nothing.

I don't mean I had trouble finding an item or two; I mean I found *nothing*. Everything God does in the work of ministry, He does through prayer. Consider:

- Prayer is the way you defeat the devil (Luke 22:32; James 4:7).
- Prayer is the way you get the lost saved (Luke 18:13).
- Prayer is the way you acquire wisdom (James 1:5).
- Prayer is the way a backslider gets restored (James 5:16–20).
- Prayer is how the saints get strengthened (Jude 20, Matthew 26:41).
- Prayer is the way we get laborers out to the mission field (Matthew 9:38).
- Prayer is how we cure the sick (James 5:13–15).
- Prayer is how we accomplish the impossible (Mark 11:23–24).

I could go on listing the myriad divine activities initiated by prayer, but I suspect you get the point. Everything we do that's worth doing; everything God wants to do in the church; everything God wants to do in your life; He has subjugated it all to one thing: Prayer. I am reminded of a little paradigm I heard years ago that embodies a crucial truth concerning our prayer lives:

What we do for the Lord is entirely dependent upon what we receive from the Lord, and what we receive from the Lord is entirely dependent upon what we are in the Lord, and what we are in the Lord is entirely dependent upon the time we spend alone with the Lord in prayer.

It is impossible for us to do or to be anything that God wants us to do or be, apart from spending time in the prayer closet.

THE POWER AND PRACTICE OF THE EARLY CHURCH

So prayer is indispensable to the work of ministry, both in our personal lives and in the life of the church. The natural question then arises: Was prayer as central to the early church? Was it as important in the beginning as we understand it to be today? The best place to answer that question is to scan the book of Acts, which tells the story of the early church.

And what we find is that Acts is a veritable handbook on prayer. Everywhere you turn, the disciples are praying—and remarkable things are happening in response. This is true from the very first chapter. Immediately following the Lord's ascension, the disciples returned to Jerusalem and congregated in an "upper room." Luke lists all the people who were present, all those who would make up the leadership and foundation of the church. Then he says, "these all with one mind were continually devoting themselves to prayer...." That was the foundation of the church; it all got started through prayer. And that was even before Pentecost!

So then, did things change when the Spirit came upon the church as described in Acts 2? Not if by "change" we mean that the church curtailed its praying. If anything, it vastly increased. As you progress through the Book of Acts from one chapter to the next, one verse to the next, all you see is prayer. You see prayer and its result in Peter's sermon (2:41); you see it again immediately following the sermon (2:43, 47); you find it following the first conflict with the Jewish religious leaders (4:24–31); you see more prayer in the selection of deacons (6:5–6). It becomes clear early on that prayer is the top priority of the early church leaders (6:4). Prayer saturates the book like salt saturates the oceans. The church prays when Peter is thrown in prison (12:5) and it's still praying when he is miraculously released (12:12). Earnest prayers are said when the church sends out Paul and Barnabas as missionaries (13:3) and equally fervent prayers are offered during the journey (14:23).

No matter where you look in the book of Acts, you see prayer. It is the hub around which the dynamic early church was moving. In the early days there was no such thing as a powerful church without prayer...just as in our day there'll never be such a thing as a powerful church without prayer.

Some may say, "Well, those were New Testament days and we're beyond that." True. But if you trace the life of the church of Jesus Christ from 2,000 years ago all the way up to this moment, you will discover that even after the New Testament canon is closed, *all* the great revivals and awakenings of church history were fueled by the power of prayer.

STRANGE TITLE, GREAT BOOK

Some time ago a friend gave me a book featuring one of the strangest titles I've ever seen. It's a book on prayer and it has taken its place alongside two shelves of other books on prayer I keep in my library. It is called *Concerts of Prayer*. With a name like that, I had no idea what to make of it. Could it be a book on how to sing our prayers to God?

The mystery cleared up soon after I started reading. The book describes the prayer movements of past generations and how God wants to move in our own generation with what author David Bryant calls "concerts of prayer." It turns out the term is taken from Matthew 18:19–20, which says, "I tell you that if two of you on earth agree about anything you ask for, it will be done for you by my Father in heaven. For where two or three come together in my name, there am I with them" (NIV). The word "concert" is another translation of the word rendered "agree." In Greek, it's the term *sumfoneo*, from which we get our English word "symphony." The term is a combination of two words, *sum* (together) and *foneo* (to sound). In other words, if two or three believers have a symphony of prayer—if two or three of them are in concert, if they sound out together before God—then God promises to be with them and He will do what they ask.

In preparing to write his book on concerts of prayer, Bryant scoured history and researched every major great awakening that has ever occurred. Guess what? At the beginning, middle, and at every other point in every awakening, there was prayer. Bryant went all the way back to the great monastic movements and the Reformation. He went back to the revival of piety that took place under Count Nicholas, Ludwig Von Zinzendorf, who lived from 1700 to 1760. He went back to the Moravian

Awakening. And as he traced all these great movements of awakening and revival and renewal, he found prayer saturating everything.

Bryant also discusses the last great awakening that occurred in America. The revival began in 1857, when a Manhattan businessman by the name of Jeremiah Lanphier sent out an invitation for people to join him at the Reform Church Consistory on Fulton Street for a noontime prayer meeting focused on revival. At the first gathering, six people showed up (out of a population of more than a million). Gradually that prayer meeting spread and by 1858 in New York City alone about six thousand people were involved in a daily, noontime prayer meeting. Tens of thousands crowded into the churches for prayer in the evenings—and ten thousand souls a week were being converted. At the same time in Chicago, almost two thousand gathered for an hour of prayer every noon. Eventually this prayer movement spread to almost all of the English-speaking world, to the mission fields and beyond. It resulted in an awakening, a spiritual revival, a time of refreshing from God in which evangelism and missions spread far and wide and the work of God went forward.

That was the last time concerts of prayer swept America and changed the face of the nation, but it's not the last time such an awakening has occurred anywhere in the world. Not so long ago, in October 1949, a group of ministers from the Hebrides Islands (situated just off the northwest coast of Scotland) met to discuss an appalling drift away from the church. The religious life of the islanders was rotten and decaying. Many congregations were reduced to a handful of elderly members. Young people between the ages of eighteen and thirty-five scarcely ever attended church functions and many churches had been abandoned. Of all places on the earth, the Hebrides Islands looked least promising for a scene of revival.

These ministers passed a resolution and made a covenant with each other that they would pray themselves out of their situation. Small groups formed to pray to confess their own lack of zeal for the things of God and to ask for His intervention. They met in churches and in barns and in homes and in open fields. Wherever two or three could gather, they met. One night in a barn meeting a young man, a church deacon, rose and read a passage from the book of Psalms—and a mighty revival broke out among the Christians. For five weeks the revival continued. When the islands' believers finally were restored to fellowship with God and filled with the Holy Spirit, revival began to spread throughout the community.

Believers brought God's revival down and men everywhere throughout the Hebrides Islands became deeply conscious that God was in their midst. Like the prophet in Isaiah chapter 6, the people suddenly became vividly aware of the awfulness of their sin. And also, like Isaiah, they abhorred that sin and turned away from it. The revival spread to Arnol, a town on one of the islands, and within forty-eight hours the town drinking house was closed, boarded up, and never reopened. How can you run a drinking house when your clientele is attending prayer meetings? The revival continued to spread and increase until it had a purging effect on the whole community.

And it all started with prayer.

A PLAN TO PRAY

A few years ago my friend Dave Burnham established Bible studies and small groups throughout the city of Akron, Ohio, and built a church of over 4,000 on the concept of small groups praying together and studying together. Maybe it's time to ask God to do something new among us, to give us a new format, a new opportunity that will make it possible for all of us to be involved in concerted prayer, accountable to each other and praying for the fire of God to fall again upon His people.

I like what one busy pastor has written about getting serious with prayer. He says this:

> Unless I'm badly mistaken, one of the main reasons so many of
> God's children don't have a significant prayer life is not so much

that we don't want to, but that we don't plan to. If you want to take a four-week vacation, you don't just get up one summer morning and say, "Hey, let's go today!" You won't have anything ready. You won't know where to go. Nothing has been planned.

But that is how many of us treat prayer. We get up day after day and realize that significant times of prayer should be a part of our life, but nothing's ever ready. We don't know where to go. Nothing has been planned. No time. No place. No procedure. And we all know that the opposite of planning is not a wonderful flow of deep, spontaneous experiences in prayer. The opposite of planning is the rut. If you don't plan a vacation you will probably stay home and watch TV. The natural, unplanned flow of spiritual life sinks to the lowest ebb of vitality. There is a race to be run and a fight to be fought. If you want renewal in your life of prayer you must plan to see it.

Therefore, my simple exhortation is this: Let us take time this very day to rethink our priorities and how prayer fits in. Make some new resolve. Try some new venture with God. Set a time. Set a place. Choose a portion of Scripture to guide you. Don't be tyrannized by the press of busy days. We all need mid-course corrections. Make this a day of turning to prayer—for the glory of God and for the fullness of your joy.[5]

We don't need new programs; we don't need one more activity. But we do need to embark together on the great adventure of prayer. Somehow we need to organize our prayer so that all of us are encouraged to join the adventure.

TRIPLE-CORD PRAYER

As I've studied the spiritual awakenings that have broken out in recent years, the nation of South Korea repeatedly comes up. Literally hundreds of thousands of people have come to Christ there and revival and renewal has spread across that war-torn land, bringing a freshness of the Spirit of God the nation has never before known. At the very core of this great move of God is prayer. Out of that spiritual renewal an idea was born that was conceived from two or three passages of Scripture. The idea was called the triple-cord prayer ministry.

Rather than trying to merge the schedules of hundreds of people in one place and at one time, someone suggested that two or three merge their schedules for even ten or fifteen minutes a week. Let them bind themselves to one another by a covenant and before God, commit themselves for at least ten minutes a week to find a place and a time to pray for the lost people they know, as well as for the ministry of their church. These small groups make it their aim before God to bring the fire of the Lord down upon His people.

I wonder what would happen in our own land if thousands of people across America committed themselves to organizing and faithfully participating in such triple-cord prayer groups? What might transpire if these believers committed themselves to pray for at least ten minutes a week for six people who are lost, two names submitted by each member of the triple-cord team? And what explosive growth might we see in our churches if these teams prayed specifically for two or three of the key ministries in their own congregations? What an adventure we might enjoy!

It's really not a far-fetched dream.

In fact...it could start with you.

Why not give it a try? Start with a three-month commitment in which you determine, by the grace of God, to find two others to join you. Identify a time and a place and commit yourselves to one another. Covenant with each other. Say to each other, "Together, we will pray and we will make prayer a priority in our lives."

If triple-cord teams would start praying like this every week all across this nation, there's no telling what God might be pleased to do. By His grace, perhaps a mighty revival would break out and begin to spread like wildfire until prayer permeates everything we do. Then God could come upon our land in a way we never dreamed of—all because we returned to the basic of praying.

TOO BUSY NOT TO PRAY

All of us are busy. Life isn't slowing down, it's speeding up, and our Day-timers reflect the fact. *Yet that is precisely why we need to take time to pray.* It is said that Martin Luther declared he had so much to do, he could not get through it without spending at least three or four hours on his knees before God each morning. Unlike him, we are tempted to think that, when life slows down, then we'll take time to pray. Jean Fleming almost stepped into that trap. Fleming wrote, "I find myself thinking, *When life settles down I'll....* But I should have learned by now that life never settles down for long. Whatever I want to accomplish, I must do with life unsettled."[6]

Oswald Chambers puts it all in perspective when he writes, "Remember, no one has time to pray; we have to take time from other things that are valuable in order to understand how necessary prayer is. The things that act like thorns and stings in our personal lives will go away instantly when we pray; we won't feel the smart any more, because we have God's point of view about them. Prayer means that we get into union with God's view of other people."[7]

Above all, we must remember that if Jesus arose early to pray on the morning after the busiest day of His life, why should we think we can do without it when busyness crowds into our own schedules? He is our model. He is our guide. Only when we follow His instructions and His example in this crucial area of prayer will we begin to discover what true adventure is all about.

Chapter Three

IT PAYS
TO PRAY

In his book *Surprise Endings*, Ron Mehl tells a powerful story about how discouragement can overpower us when long-time prayers just don't seem to be answered. It's a true account which took place just after World War II:

Roger Simms, hitchhiking his way home, would never forget the date—May 7. His heavy suitcase made Roger tired. He was anxious to take off his army uniform once and for all. Flashing the hitchhiking sign to the on-coming car, he lost hope when he saw it was a black, sleek new Cadillac. To his surprise the car stopped. The passenger door opened. He ran toward the car, tossed his suitcase in the back, and thanked the handsome, well-dressed man as he slid in the front seat.

"Going home for keeps?"

"Sure am," Roger responded.

"Well, you're in luck if you're going to Chicago."

"Not quite that far. Do you live in Chicago?"

"I have a business there. My name is Hanover."

After talking about many things, Roger, a Christian, felt a compulsion to witness to this fiftyish, apparently successful businessman about Christ. But he kept putting it off, till he realized he was just thirty minutes from his home. It was now or never. So, Roger cleared his throat, "Mr. Hanover, I would like to talk to you about something very important." He then proceeded to explain the way of salvation, ultimately asking Mr. Hanover if he would like to receive Christ as his Savior. To Roger's astonishment the Cadillac pulled over to the side of the road. Roger thought he was going to be ejected from the car. But the businessman bowed his head and received Christ, then thanked Roger, "This is the greatest thing that has ever happened to me."

Five years went by, Roger married, had a two-year-old boy, and a business of his own. Packing his suitcase for a business trip to Chicago, he found the small, white business card Hanover had given him five years before.

In Chicago he looked up Hanover Enterprises. A receptionist told him it was impossible to see Mr. Hanover, but he could see Mrs. Hanover. A little confused as to what was going on, he was ushered into a lovely office and found himself facing a keen-eyed woman in her fifties. She extended her hand, "You knew my husband?"

Roger told her how her husband had given him a ride when hitchhiking home after the war.

"Can you tell me when that was?"

"It was May 7, five years ago, the day I was discharged from the army."

"Anything special about that day?"

Roger hesitated. Should he mention his witness? Since he had come so far, he might as well take the plunge. "Mrs. Hanover, I explained the gospel. He pulled over to the side of the road and wept against the steering wheel. He gave his life to Christ that day."

Explosive sobs shook her body. Getting a grip on herself, she sobbed, "I had prayed for my husband's salvation for years. I believed God would save him."

"And," said Roger, "Where is your husband, Mrs. Hanover?"

"He's dead," she wept, struggling with words. "He was in a car crash after he let you out of the car. He never got home. You see—I thought God had not kept His promise." Sobbing uncontrollably, she added, "I stopped living for God five years ago because I thought He had not kept His word![1]

Mrs. Hanover's case is an extreme one, but in one sense it is not unusual. Many of us have been praying for someone or something for months, years, and even decades, and still we do not see the answer to our prayers. That can get discouraging.

The Lord knows that, so He takes great care to teach us about the danger of discouragement in prayer. He was so concerned about this connection between prayer and discouragement that He told not only one, but two parables to highlight the problem. I do not know of any other instance in the preaching of our Lord where He told two different stories to teach such a similar lesson. Let's first consider the stories, then see what we can learn from them.

DIFFERENT STORIES, SAME LESSON

The first parable is found in Luke 11:5–8, immediately after Luke gives his version of what is commonly called the Lord's Prayer:

> Suppose one of you shall have a friend, and shall go to him at midnight, and say to him, "Friend, lend me three loaves; for a friend of mine has come to me from a journey, and I have nothing to set before him"; and from inside he shall answer and say, "Do not bother me; the door has already been shut and my children and I are in bed; I cannot get up and give you *anything*." I

tell you, even though he will not get up and give him *anything* because he is his friend, yet because of his persistence he will get up and give him as much as he needs.

The second passage is found in Luke 18:1–8. Note the similarities of plot with the earlier story:

Now He was telling them a parable to show that at all times they ought to pray and not to lose heart, saying, "There was in a certain city a judge who did not fear God, and did not respect man. And there was a widow in that city, and she kept coming to him, saying, 'Give me legal protection from my opponent.' And for a while he was unwilling; but afterward he said to himself, 'Even though I do not fear God nor respect man, yet because this widow bothers me, I will give her legal protection, lest by continually coming she wear me out.'"

And the Lord said, "Hear what the unrighteous judge said; now shall not God bring about justice for His elect, who cry to Him day and night, and will He delay long over them? I tell you that He will bring about justice for them speedily. However, when the Son of Man comes, will He find faith on the earth?"

Jesus often used stories to make points clear, points which lie at the very core of the Christian faith. When He told a story, you can be sure it was to drive home some critical lesson. We ought not to be surprised, therefore, that Jesus taught two parables specifically to teach men *not to be discouraged in their prayer lives*. It was as if Jesus said, "I want to tell you some stories to keep you from losing heart when you pray. Prayer is far too important to allow something like that to happen!"

Prayer is the kind of exercise that can lead to discouragement if we're not careful. Some of you reading this chapter are discouraged right now, because you keep trying to pray but you can't be consistent with it. Some of you are discouraged because you pray every day and still God has not answered your request. I, too, have fought discouragement in praying. I believe that any honest Christian who deals with life openly will confess to periods of discouragement when he has prayed and it seems as if God were asleep or on vacation or just not there. If we're not careful, discouragement can slip in like a fog and chill our prayer lives.

That's why Jesus told these two stories. They teach us several things about prayer that, if properly understood, will keep us from growing disheartened.

THE CIRCUMSTANCES OF THE ONE WHO PRAYS

When the disciples went to Jesus in Luke 11 and asked Him to teach them to pray, Jesus responded with His first story. He told them of a man who found himself one day at the end of his resources, faced with a claim that he could not meet—unless he could obtain help from an outside source.

Our circumstance in life is like that of this man. We will become men and women of prayer only when we recognize our desperate need. The woman in Luke 18 is just like the man. She began to beg the judge for justice, believing she could not live without it. Our own prayers can lead to discouragement unless we see ourselves as this woman—praying at midnight, in desperate need, before the only One in the universe who can meet that need.

This is one of the most difficult things about prayer, especially in a culture like ours. Humanism is the doctrine of the day and it infects all levels of society. Humanism in its rawest form is the antithesis of the Christian gospel. It teaches that we do not need God because we ourselves are god. It says that we can be the masters of our fate, the captains of our soul.

Prayer stabs at the heart of that idea. God teaches us that we are dependent upon Him, not because He wishes to lord it over us, but because it is true. Many today refuse to accept that; they consider it an indication of weakness. More than one critic has said religion is nothing but a crutch for emotionally weak people.

But a personal relationship with Jesus Christ is not a crutch; it is the irreducible minimum of life. Jesus said to the Pharisees, "You refuse to come to me *to have life*" (John 5:40, NIV, emphasis added). Coming to Jesus is life itself! Anyone who has not come to understand this has not come to learn the basic principle of prayer. One reason why prayer is so hard for us is that prayer forces us to admit our own spiritual impotence. Its very existence shouts that God is the only source that can make us all we ought to be. God insists through His Word that until we come to Him as the widow came to the judge and as the man came to his friend, we will never know either prayer or power in our lives.

Bill Hybels, pastor of Willow Creek Community Church in Chicago and a man I deeply admire, admits in his book *Too Busy Not to Pray*, "Prayer has not always been my strong suit. For many years, even as senior pastor of a large church, I knew more about prayer than I ever practiced in my own life. I have a racehorse temperament, and the tugs of self-sufficiency and self-reliance are very real to me. I didn't want to get off the fast track long enough to find out what prayer is all about."[2] Eventually God "cured" him of this deception and Bill started acting on the truth:

> It is hard for God to release his power in your life when you put your hands in your pockets and say, "I can handle it on my own." If you do that, don't be surprised if one day you get the nagging feeling that the tide of battle has shifted against you and that you're fairly powerless to do anything about it.
>
> Prayerless people cut themselves off from God's prevailing power, and the frequent result is the familiar feeling of being

overwhelmed, overrun, beaten down, pushed around, defeated. Surprising numbers of people are willing to settle for lives like that. Don't be one of them. Nobody has to live like that. Prayer is the key to unlocking God's prevailing power in your life.[3]

Now, we can either take this by faith because God said it in His Word, or God will teach us this lesson through the difficulties of life. Do we realize how little there is between us and the widow at midnight? Just one snap of God's fingers and we're standing outside the judge's door. Many of us have learned this the hard way. We've watched as God has taken our success and turned it into failure so we could become a real success for God. No one can be big in his own eyes and big in the plans of God at the same time.

These parables teach us that we must come to God as did the widow and as did the man, recognizing our inadequacy before God. Yet this isn't "worm theology." This is not, "poor me, I can't do anything." While it is true that without Christ we can do nothing (John 15:5), the flip side is that "I can do all things through Him who strengthens me" (Philippians 4:13). When we keep these two truths in perspective, we will be ready to become all that God wants us to be.

THE CONFLICT OF THE ONE WHO PRAYS

The main characters in these two stories are people who are desperately fighting for survival. Jesus does not mean that we have to overcome divine resistance to our best interests, but He does mean that prayer is a forceful and agonizing activity of the will. Jesus Himself agonized in prayer.

Joseph Parker, the British preacher, once wrote, "Prayers are battles." Prayer was the battlefield of our Lord's life upon which He won all His victories. As Hebrews 5:7 reminds us, "In the days of His flesh...He offered up both prayers and supplications with loud crying and tears."

Luke tells us that in the Garden of Gethsemane just prior to His arrest, Jesus knelt down to pray "and being in agony He was praying very fervently; and His sweat became like drops of blood, falling down upon the ground" (Luke 22:44). Prayer is conflict.

Watch the woman banging on the door: "Will you hear me?" Listen to the man imploring to be heard: "Please, friend, won't you help me?" Prayer is conflict. It is battle. It is war.

The passive idea we often have about prayer has no place in the Word of God. Prayer is work, the hardest work you will ever do. It is grueling labor. It is agonizing. It is coming to God and coming to grips with the realities of your life.

Too often in our prayers we merely *mention* our needs. There is no urgency at all. But that kind of praying doesn't tend to get a lot accomplished. When my children were young and wanted permission for something, they didn't just "mention" it. In the same way, when you want something from your Father in heaven, don't just "mention" it. Come to God in persistent, importunate prayer.

Oswald Chambers wrote, "Men always ought to pray, and not lose heart. Jesus also taught the disciples the prayer of patience. If you are right with God and God delays the answer to your prayer, don't misjudge Him. Don't think of Him as an unkind friend, or an unnatural father, or an unjust judge, but keep at it. Your prayer will certainly be answered, for 'everyone who asks receives.' Pray and do not cave in. Your heavenly Father will explain it all one day. He cannot just yet because He is developing your character."[4]

I have a friend whose father did not become a believer until he was sixty-two years old. For more than thirty years this man's godly wife prayed for his salvation, but without any apparent effect. Then three things happened within weeks of each other, seemingly "by coincidence," that changed everything. And at least two of the three events in question were not "good."

First, this man's body started breaking down due to job-related stress. He had always been very healthy and this unanticipated turn of events worried him as nothing ever had. Suddenly he was confronted with his mortality and the scene frightened him.

Second, he started attending church regularly for the first time in his life. His wife was growing increasingly immobile from arthritis and needed constant help in getting around. He had no particular interest in attending, but because he loved his wife and she didn't want to miss church, he took her.

Third, the church had just welcomed a new pastor whose speaking style attracted the man. The former pastor was outstanding, but the man had heard him for years and was "innoculated" against whatever he had to say. The new pastor had a fresh style which penetrated the man's heart. And during one service when the Spirit was convicting him and drawing him to God, the man gave his life to Christ.

Now note—God didn't answer this woman's prayers for more than thirty years, and when He did answer them, He used job-related stress, arthritis, and a change in pastors to get the job done. Would salvation have come to this man without his wife's persistent prayers? What would have happened had she stopped praying fifteen years into her battle? No one can say for certain, but I do know one thing for sure: This woman is glad she didn't give up. And so is her husband.

George Mueller, the great prayer warrior, once said, "The great fault of the children of God is, they do not continue in prayer: they do not go on praying; they do not persevere. If they desire anything for God's glory, they should pray until they get it. Oh how good, and kind, and gracious, and condescending is the One with Whom we have to do! He has given me, unworthy as I am, immeasurably above all I had asked or thought!"[5]

THE CONCERN OF THE ONE WHO PRAYS

Acute need is the motivating factor in the stories of both Luke 11 and 18. The man requests bread while the woman asks for "justice," probably in a dispute about money. Both requests are born out of deep needs in the real world.

Jesus is teaching us that prayer is not just for church on Sunday. It is not offered only before some shrine. Prayer wears denim work clothes. It is about day-to-day living. The issues we pray about stem from needs in our daily experience. Prayer is about everyday things, about bread and about money.

We must never make prayer into some spiritual, make-believe game that does not focus on the real needs that confront us. I've been in prayer meetings in which the prayers offered made me wonder whether the people lived on the same planet I do. Oswald Chambers once wrote, "Some of the things that we pray about are as absurd as if we prayed, 'O Lord, take me out of this room,' and then refused to go."[6]

How often have we prayed something like, "O Lord, be with Cousin Billy now in a special way"? Have we stopped to consider what it is we're requesting? Imagine that you are a parent who is preparing to leave your children with a new babysitter. Would you dream of saying, "O Betsy, I ask now that you would be with my children in a special way"? No way. You would say, "Betsy, the kids need to be in bed by 9 P.M. They can have one snack before their baths, and please make sure they finish their homework. You can reach us at this number if there's any problem. Any questions before we go?" We are very specific with our requests and instructions for our babysitters. We want them to know specifics. It should be no different with prayer.

Prayer is about real-world concerns, spoken in real-world language. God does not want us to shift into a stained-glass prayer voice to address Him. Prayer comes out of this world, the workaday world of houses and cars and grass and sewer lines and schools and janitors and the IRS. Prayer is about bread. Prayer is about money. Prayer is about a judge in conflict. It's about feeding unexpected company in the middle of the night when your cupboard is bare and the stores are closed. That's what

God teaches us through these two parables. The necessity of prayer springs out of needs in the real world.

THE CHALLENGE OF THE ONE WHO PRAYS

Prayer is a challenging effort, a constant reminder of the problems we face.

Sometimes it seems as if God is asleep and He does not hear us. Prayer can often appear to be the most useless and fruitless experience. Oswald Chambers noted, "Prayer to us is not practical, it is stupid, and until we do see that prayer is stupid, that is, stupid from the ordinary, natural, common sense point of view, we will never pray. 'It is absurd to think that God is going to alter things in answer to prayer.' But that is what Jesus says He will do. It sounds stupid, but it is a stupidity based on His redemption. The reason that our prayers are not answered is that we are not stupid enough to believe what Jesus says."[7]

We must guard ourselves from these feelings that prayer is useless, as well as from the changing moods that interrupt our prayer discipline. When we receive no answer, we must go on praying. Even though the judge would not listen to the woman when she first began to pray, and even though it seemed as if nothing was happening when she did pray, all the while something *was* happening: Resistance in the heart of the judge was breaking down, bit by bit. The woman, of course, knew nothing of this. She wasn't aware that anything was going on until the judge ultimately responded. Yet all the time she was praying, something *was* happening.

We err when we judge our prayers solely by what we can see happening around us. Prayer is a matter of faith. Prayer is taking God at His word. Prayer is understanding God's promise that if we pray, He will work. And we must keep on praying even when we cannot see what He is doing. We do not see into the world in which God lives, but He definitely sees into ours, as the following personal testimony by Spencer January attests:

It was 1945, and the U.S. Army's 35th Infantry Division, of which I was a twenty-four year-old member, was pushing through the woods and towns in the Rhineland region of West Germany. As I and my comrades were cautiously making our way through a thickly wooded area, word came that the company ahead of us had been badly shot up by the enemy and that Company I was to replace them.

When my company arrived on the scene, I was appalled by the grimness of the situation. Only a handful of wounded, bleeding soldiers hiding behind a large stone house at the edge of the woods had survived. The route to Ossenburg had been completely blockaded. "God," I prayed desperately, thinking of my wife and little son back home, "You've got to do something... please do something, God!"

Moments later, the order was given to advance. Just as the soldier ahead of me took a step, something to the left caught my eye. I stopped and stared in amazement. A cloud—a long, fluffy, white cloud—had appeared instantly out of nowhere, obscuring the Germans' line of fire. Taking advantage of this miraculous turn of events, I and my fellow soldiers bolted into the clearing and ran for our lives. Safe in the sheltering woods on the other side of the clearing, my pulse pounding in my ears, I hid behind a tree and exclaimed, "This has to be God! I'm going to see what happens now."

I watched closely as the last American soldier frantically raced toward my comrades in the woods. I will never forget what happened next. The instant the soldier scrambled to safety, the cloud vanished! Just like that. Poof! It was gone.

The Germans, thinking they still had us pinned down behind the stone house on the other side of the field, radioed its position to their artillery. Minutes later, the house was blown to bits.

Two weeks later, a letter arrived from my mother back in Dallas, Texas. "Son, what in the world was the matter on the morning of March 9?" she asked. "You remember Mrs. Tankersly from our church? Well, she called me that morning and said the Lord had awakened her at one o'clock in the night and said, 'Spencer is in serious trouble. Get up now and pray for him!' Mrs. Tankersly said she interceded for you until six o'clock the next morning. She told me that the last thing she prayed before getting off her knees was, 'Lord, whatever danger Spencer is in, just cover him with a cloud!'"[8]

We will often discover that when God finally answers our prayers, His answer came in a moment in time but was being prepared over a long period of time. We did not know it, but the preparation was going on all the while we were praying. As Spencer January (now 76) says, "God loves us and hears every prayer we pray, whether it's a sinner asking Him for mercy and forgiveness, or someone crying out to Him for miraculous protection or for healing. In Psalm 91, God promises: 'He will call upon me, and I will answer him; I will be with him in trouble; I will deliver him and honor him. With long life will I satisfy him, and show him my salvation.' That's God's Word to you and me. And I am living proof that He keeps His promises!"[9]

THE CONSTANCY OF THE ONE WHO PRAYS

Constancy is the main point of both stories in Luke 11 and 18. They are intended to teach us that no matter what we observe outwardly, no matter what seems to be coming back to us through our sensory perceptions, the fundamental truth of the Christian life is wrapped up in our prayer to God. By our praying we are giving evidence that we have committed ourselves to Him and that even though we can't see what He is doing, we know He is doing something and we will not abort that process by ceasing to pray. We will not lose hope; we will not get discouraged; we will continue to pray.

I read somewhere that the greatest blessing of prayer is not in receiving an answer, but rather in being the kind of person God can trust with the answer. It is something like athletics. It is good to win the game, but it is better to be the kind of healthy, coordinated person who can play the game. The excitement of victory will fade, but the blessing of a strong, healthy body remains. We rejoice at answered prayer, but we should rejoice more that God has brought us to the place spiritually where He can afford to answer our prayers.

So much of the time we're all wrapped up in the product. God isn't; He's wrapped up in the process. We're all looking for the answer; God is looking for the person who will pray, even when he cannot see the answer. It is only that kind of person whom God can ultimately trust with the answer. If we are short-fused people who will pray only when we immediately get what we want, then God can't trust us with any big answers to our prayers. But if we are consistent men and women who take God at His word,

who believe that prayer changes things,

who will pray without ceasing,

who will not lose heart at our praying,

who day after day will pray no matter what seems to be happening around us,

who keep trusting God,

then there will come a time when God will say, "I can answer that believer's prayer because that's a person who can handle the answer."

PRAYING TO THE ONLY ONE WHO GIVES MEANING

Years ago when I needed a break from a hectic schedule, my family took a quick trip up to Lake Arrowhead. I just walked around in the mountains. It was a wonderful, refreshing recovery time. Somehow when you go to the mountains, you clear your head. It's no accident that the Old Testament says, "I will lift up mine eyes unto the hills from whence cometh my help." Something happens to you when you go to the mountains. I don't know what it is, but it's wonderful. I'm so fortunate to live where I do. God created the mountains and the ocean as therapy for His people, and I'm just a short distance from each one.

As I walked, I thought. I understood, maybe for the first time, why it is so critical to develop a strong and deep relationship with Jesus Christ. I realized there is simply no other relationship on earth that can meet our ultimate need. This is no fault of the persons to whom we are related, but simply reflects how we were created. As Augustine said to God, "You have made us for Yourself, and our hearts are restless until they find their rest in You."

You say, "That's unfair!" No, that's life. That's the way life is. Life on planet Earth is ultimately a disappointment. I'm not being a pessimist; I'm being a realist. If we put all our hopes and pour all our lives into human relationships, there *will* come a time when they end up bringing to us less than what we'd hoped for.

I have four children into whom I have poured my life. But those children are changing. Do you know what happens to a father who pours his life into his daughter? Some day, another man comes along and pirates her love away. You know, that doesn't seem right! Do you know what happens to a father who pours his life into his son and his athletic career and plays ball with him and watches him grow and develop? Some day that boy graduates and he goes to the ends of the earth to play where his dad can't even watch him. That doesn't mean the relationship is bad. It just means it changes and can't give back everything you hoped it would.

Do you know what I wrote down that day as I walked around Lake Arrowhead? Here it is: "Jesus Christ, the same yesterday, today and forever."

Why is it that we have such a hard time praying to the only One who can bring meaning to our lives? The primary culprit is the enemy of our souls, who wants to keep us from developing a relationship that he knows will bring joy and satisfaction to us. O, that we would resist him and instead "draw near with confidence to the throne of grace, that we may receive mercy and may find grace to help in time of need" (Hebrews 4:16)!

By the grace of God, we need to determine that we are going to keep on praying. Only through prayer will we become the kind of people God can trust with the real answers. Only in the process of praying will we find the meaning of life for which everyone seeks: A dynamic, personal relationship with the Creator, the living Lord, the Babe of Bethlehem, the Savior of the Cross, the resurrection morning Victor, the only One who is life to us.

DON'T LOSE HEART!

I learned many things from my professors in seminary. My all-time favorite was Howard Hendricks, the head of the department under which I studied. He is a tremendous communicator and a great man of God. He taught us much by his descriptive language and his unique way of communicating. But one of the greatest lessons I learned from Dr. Hendricks had nothing to do with the lesson of the day. I can't remember the year; I don't even know what class I was in. But he came in one day and, through tears, said, "Gentlemen, I want to tell you something. My seventy-five year old father received Jesus Christ as his Savior. That might not be meaningful to you unless I tell you that for forty years, I have prayed for his salvation. And after forty years, God finally said yes."

No wonder "Jesus told his disciples a parable to show them that they should always pray and not give up."

It pays to pray.

It pays not to give up.

Certainly discouragement sometimes comes with prayer, but

remember this: There will *always* be discouragement without prayer! Discouragement follows prayerlessness like winter follows fall. But when we choose to continue praying, even through a long and barren winter, eventually spring arrives and with it new life. And at that point, discouragement has no choice but to find somewhere else to live.

Part Two

DIGGING FOR GOLD

Chapter Four

A ROADMAP
FOR PRAYER

F rom the beginning of the Bible to its conclusion, we see absolute
evidence that God answers prayer. Things that we think are
impossible, God does when people pray.

Prayer has won victories over fire and air and earth and water.

Prayer opened the Red Sea.

Prayer brought water from the rock and bread from heaven.

Prayer made the sun stand still.

Prayer brought fire from the sky on Elijah's sacrifice.

Prayer overthrew armies and healed the sick.

Prayer raised the dead.

Prayer has paved the way for the conversion of millions of people.

When we pray, we align ourselves with the purposes of God and tap
into the power of the Almighty. Because we pray, God works through us
in ways that He wouldn't otherwise. God has made certain things dependent upon prayer, things that will never be done unless we pray. Could
God do whatever He chooses without our prayer? Of course. But God
has determined that He will use the prayers of His people to accomplish
His purposes on this earth. When we do not pray, we limit what God
might do in our lives.

Some may not like the sound of this, but if it were not true, what could James mean when he writes, "You do not have, because you do not ask God" (James 4:2, NIV)? Why would Paul ask some friends to "pray for us that the message of the Lord may spread rapidly and be honored…pray that we may be delivered from wicked and evil men" (2 Thessalonians 3:1–2, NIV), if he did not believe their prayers had the power to change his circumstances? Both James and Paul believed that God might well withhold His hand of blessing from them if they neglected to pray. Since they wanted all the blessing available to them, they not only prayed themselves, they recruited others to pray for them. They never wanted to limit what God might be pleased to do in and through them by failing to pray.

If we want all the blessing God has available to give us, we, too, must pray. But *how* are we to pray? With what kind of attitude are we to bow our heads? With what kind of expectation? With what strength of hope? How much depends on us, and how much on God?

THE GREAT DEBATE

Christians over the years have been divided in regard to the sovereignty of God and how it affects the purpose and power of prayer. The two major groups are called "Calvinists" and "Arminians." Calvinists are known to be very committed to the sovereignty of God; He's totally in charge. Arminians stress the free will of man; God will do only so much, depending on how we respond to Him. (Whenever folks ask me what I am, I tell them I'm a Calminian.)

I remember reading about George Whitefield, a Calvinist, and John Wesley, an Arminian. One evening after a very strenuous day, the two of them returned to the boarding house where they were staying. After preparing to retire for the evening, each of them knelt beside his bed to pray. Whitefield, the Calvinist, prayed like this: "Lord, we thank Thee for all those with whom we spoke today, and we rejoice that their lives and their destinies are entirely in Thy hands. Honor our efforts according to Thy perfect will. Amen." He rose from his knees and got into bed.

Wesley, who had hardly gotten past the invocation of his prayer by this time, looked up and said, "Mr. Whitefield, is this where your Calvinism leads you?" Then he bowed his head and went on praying. Whitefield went to sleep and when he awoke about two hours later, there was Wesley, still on his knees beside the bed. Whitefield got up and went around to where Wesley was kneeling, only to find him asleep. He shook him by the shoulder and said, "Mr. Wesley, is this where your Arminianism leads you?"[1]

What is the balance between Calvinism (which says it's all up to God) and Arminianism (which says most of it's up to us)? How do we discover God's part in prayer and our part? There is no better teaching on that subject than the Lord's Prayer. It is perfectly in balance. It teaches us who He is and who we are, and how we are to come to Him in prayer.

THE BEST KNOWN PRAYER IN THE WORLD

The prayer we know as "The Lord's Prayer" came from the Lord Jesus in direct response to His disciples' request: "Lord, teach us to pray." It has always fascinated me that they never asked Jesus to teach them to preach. They never asked Him to teach them to give or to witness. Perhaps, like us, the disciples were often at a loss when it came to communicating with the Almighty. The Lord's Prayer is the model Jesus designed to show them how to pray, and it has lost none of its power after almost two thousand years.

There are just sixty-six words in the Lord's Prayer, but it is the most well-known prayer in history. There is nothing like it in all the literature of the world, nothing remotely approaching its majesty and power and insight. It may be brief, but it packs a wallop. As we study it and delve into its meaning, we'll learn some of the greatest theology we will ever acquire. It is not too much to say that *this prayer is at the very heart of who God is and what He longs for His children to be.*

Before we take apart this prayer to discover its hidden jewels, let's take some time to consider it as a unit. Let's start by reading through it from start to finish:

Our Father who art in heaven
Hallowed be Thy name.
Thy kingdom come.
Thy will be done,
On earth as it is in heaven.
Give us this day our daily bread.
And forgive us our debts, as we also have forgiven our debtors.
And do not lead us into temptation, but deliver us from evil.
For Thine is the kingdom, and the power, and the glory, forever.
Amen (Matthew 6:9–13).

Notice the emphasis on God in the first three petitions: *Thy* name, *Thy* kingdom, *Thy* will. Then notice the second part of the prayer and its emphasis on the poverty of man: Give *us*, forgive *us*, deliver *us*. Then see how the prayer comes full circle by ending with a tight focus on God once more: *Thy* kingdom, *Thy* power, *Thy* glory. God has all the glory and all the power and all the majesty, and you and I have all the needs and all the wants and all the poverty. He's got everything; we have nothing. It's wonderful to come with empty hands to the One who is able to give us everything we need. That's what this prayer is all about and what it will teach us if we strive to learn its secrets.

A ROADMAP FOR PRAYER

The Lord's Prayer is a roadmap for us to use when we pray. It's like driving down a highway dotted to one side with signposts.

As we pass the first intersection, we are reminded that we need to acknowledge and give *praise* to God: "Our Father who art in heaven, hallowed be Thy name."

In just three days, I will be celebrating my 55th birthday, and I want to thank You, Lord, for allowing me another year of life on this earth. I know that You have been gracious to me and have helped me, and I am so thankful for all You have done. Yesterday I received a wonderful birthday card from Dick DeNure. I was very low yesterday, and then this card came to my desk, and in it was this note:

Happy birthday, and what a year it's been. Healed from a terrible disease, sold a house and built a new one (No mean feat in these challenging times), had a son do so remarkably well on the football field and win a county championship, had a daughter just get married, had a radio program grow to major proportions, got a son and daughter-in-law back to California and into a new home, preached wonderful sermons each Sunday several times to a huge number of people, led a vibrant school system, pre-school through college, managed a complex system of ministries from in-home Bible studies to missionaries throughout the world, and the list of wonderful blessings and marvelous use of gifts goes on and on. And this from the perspective of one who just sees a small part of what is happening from a seat in the congregation. It's clear, like your namesake, you are a man after God's own heart. May this next year be as incredible as the last one. We do indeed have an awesome God!

Lord, how awesome You are to give such encouragement to me through one of Your children. I cannot say that all of the pain left when I read this note, but I can say that it did help me to have perspective on what You are doing and to realize that You have been incredibly good to me and to my whole family!

We keep driving, and at the next intersection we see another sign that says we are to pray over our *priorities* and bring them into line with God's: "Thy kingdom come. Thy will be done on earth as it is in heaven."

The next sign reminds us that the God we have worshiped, the God who is in control of our life, is the same God who wants to *provide* for our daily needs. So we pray, "Give us this day our daily bread."

As we keep moving, we see a big sign that says *personal relationships*: "Forgive us our debts as we forgive our debtors." The people we know come flooding into our minds, so we take inventory of how our relationships are going with them. If any of them need repair, we stop to get it done.

At the next intersection there's another signpost: "Lead us not into temptation, but deliver us from evil." Here we are reminded that the God who provides is also the God who *protects*, so we pray to God for His protection and deliverance.

As we approach the final exit, we see one last signpost: "For Thine is the kingdom and the power and the glory forever. Amen." What a tremendous *promise* this is! To know that the God to whom we pray is an everlasting King with the power to do whatever pleases Him and a glory that outshines a million suns in a billion trillion galaxies! It ought to take away our breath to realize that *this* is the God who invites us to bring our worship and our requests to Him.

As you traveled down this sacred highway, did you notice that the Lord's Prayer covers every relationship we have with God? When we say, "Our Father," that's the Father/child relationship. When we say, "Hallowed be Thy name," that's the Deity/worshiper relationship. When we say, "Thy kingdom come," that's the Sovereign/subject relationship. When we say, "Thy will be done," that's the Master/servant relationship. When we say, "Give us this day our daily bread," that's the Benefactor/beneficiary relationship. When we say, "Forgive us our trespasses," that's the Savior/sinner relationship. When we say, "Lead us not into temptation," that's the Guide/pilgrim relationship. And when we say,

"For Thine is the kingdom, and the power, and the glory, forever," that's the Creator/creature relationship.

Whenever we pray according to the model of this prayer, we are emphasizing our right relationship to God in heaven. This prayer works amazingly well as a reliable guide for life. That is why I say that *this prayer is at the very heart of who God is and what He longs for His children to be.*

KNOWING DOESN'T NECESSARILY MEAN DOING

But knowing we should pray doesn't always translate into action, does it? Most of us have heard more than a few sermons on the subject of prayer. Maybe we've read a few books. I probably have a hundred books on prayer in my library; I know a lot *about* prayer. But the Lord has been teaching me in the past decade of my life that prayer isn't something we learn by listening to sermons or reading books alone. Prayer is something we learn by praying! We cannot learn to pray only by hearing about it.

As Andrew Murray said, "Reading a book about prayer, listening to lectures and talking about it is very good, but it won't teach you to pray. You get nothing without exercise, without practice. I might listen for a year to a professor of music playing the most beautiful music, but that won't teach me to play an instrument."[2]

Three habits will help us to ready our hearts and minds for a meaningful time of prayer:

ANTICIPATE - God our heavenly Father, loving Counselor, peace-giving Friend, and gentle Shepherd, is coming to see us. His arms are laden with gifts that will change our lives. Let the thought of this fill your day…. The Lord is there…what a mind-boggling thought. The Almighty God, Creator of the universe, has come to spend time with you. You are the recipient of His undivided attention. He has a plan-blueprint of your life, written in the palm of His hand. Remind yourself before going to bed at night—the Lord is here!

ACKNOWLEDGE - As you begin your devotional time, acknowledge that God is present. It may be helpful to say something like this: I come to be with You this morning, Lord. Thank You for Your faithfulness and constant presence with me. Thank You for taking time to spend with me. I offer myself to You for this important interval together. For some, it helps to imagine Jesus sitting in a chair nearby, ready to speak and listen. His presence is as real as the chair in front of us.

ACCLIMATE - First, be comfortable, but not too comfortable. In Scripture, people bowed, stood, lay down, sat, or knelt when praying. We want to be in a posture that requires little thought. Richard Foster suggests that we place our palms upon our knees to symbolize a heart of receptivity and expectation.[3]

In talking with hundreds of Christians about this subject in casual conversations, I have discovered a deep and abiding frustration on the part of many of God's people when it comes to prayer. Some who have been Christians for many years frankly confess that prayer has been a struggle from the very beginning. Andrew Murray commented that "if we do not learn how to pray when we are younger, we will stumble at it all of our lives."[4] I must confess that even as a pastor, there have been many years when prayer has been a great struggle for me. Why is it that some people pray with such great power and fervor while some of us struggle with it all our lives?

The disciples who lived and walked with Jesus had many of the same frustrations you and I have. Why else would they have come to Jesus one day and said to Him, "Lord, please show us how to pray like you pray"? In Luke's rendition of the prayer, Jesus answered, "When you pray, say this..." and then He gave us this prayer. It by no means exhausts everything we might say to God, but it does provide an outline for prayer that gets us started in the right direction. If we were to put this outline prayer in outline form, it might look like this:

I. Emphasis on God
  A. Praise (6:9)
  B. Priorities (6:10)
II. Emphasis on us
  A. Provision (6:11)
  B. Personal relationships (6:12)
  C. Protection (6:13a)
III. Emphasis on God
  A. Promise (6:13b)

As we dig deeper into this rich vein of divine ore, we'll follow the contours of this simple outline. And as we do so, let's be careful to remember that the purpose of our expedition is not merely to admire the nuggets we uncover, but to bring them into the full light of day where we can appropriate them for our own use. Gold is beautiful, but it's also amazingly useful. It spends! It purchases! It has great practical value as a currency. Let's make sure that we honor our Lord's words in His prayer by enjoying them fully for both their beauty and their usefulness.

DON'T BE A HYPOCRITE

Immediately before Jesus taught the disciples the Lord's Prayer, He gave them some preliminary instructions. In Matthew 6:5 the Lord says, "when you pray, you are not to be as the hypocrites; for they love to stand and pray in the synagogues and on the street corners, in order to be seen by men. Truly I say to you, they have their reward in full."

In the Jewish culture of Jesus' time, religious people prayed every three hours, at 3:00, 6:00, 9:00, etc. The hypocrites used to plan their day so that they would be in the busiest part of the village when it was time to pray. When they stopped, raised their arms, and prayed flowery, fluent prayers, people around them would say, "My, what wonderful, godly people they must be."

The Lord Jesus tells us not to be like that, for hypocritical praying focuses on position instead of piety. Those who love to pray in public so they can parade their piety are not following the will of God. The great preacher Dr. G. Campbell Morgan once said, "We Christians should keep Lent within our hearts and everlasting Easter on our face." He meant that we should not parade something false. We should always be genuine when we come to God in prayer. Oswald Chambers said it like this:

> The primary thought in the area of religion is—keep your eyes on God, not on people. Your motivation should not be the desire to be known as a praying person. Find an inner room in which to pray where no one even knows you are praying, shut the door, and talk to God in secret. Have no motivation other than to know your Father in heaven. It is impossible to carry on your life as a disciple without definite times of secret prayer.[5]

This doesn't mean that public praying is wrong. Some groups have taken these words of our Lord and have used them to forbid group praying. That is not what He meant (note the many times the Gospels show Him praying in public, as well as the many group prayers we find in the book of Acts). There is a place for public prayers, but they must be genuine and they must never take the place of our private praying. One man has written:

> Have you ever seen a bright blue iceberg? In Alaska I stared in awe at a mountain lake filled with beautiful blue icebergs that had broken off Portage Glacier. Immediately my mind went back to an article in a *Family Time* magazine that compared our secret praying to an iceberg. The "Absolutely No Boating" on the edge of the lake reminded me that eight-ninths of the bulk of an iceberg is below the waterline—out of sight. Only one-ninth is visible above

the surface. The next day at our prayer seminar in Anchorage I explained how prayer should be like those icebergs, with about one-ninth showing in our public group praying and eight-ninths out of sight in our secret closets.[6]

We should not be like the hen who goes into a secret place to lay her eggs, but by all her cackling announces where she is and what she's doing. Jesus tells us to enter into our closet and to pray to our Father who is in secret. What a sweet instruction this is! As Andrew Murray exhorts us, "O do what Jesus says: Just shut the door, and pray to thy Father which is in secret. Is it not wonderful? To be able to go alone with God, the infinite God. And then to look up and say: My Father!"[7]

DON'T BE A HEATHEN

Second, the Lord Jesus tells us, "when you pray, do not use vain repetitions as the heathen do, for they think they will be heard for their many words. Therefore, do not be like them, for your Father knows the things you have need of before you ask Him" (Matthew 6:7–8).

Someone once said that "one sentence burdened with the heart's desire is dearer to God than an hour's rehearsing of words and phrases with no longing behind them." God doesn't want vain repetitions; He wants real communication. When we pray, He wants us to put our heart into it.

Dr. Reuben Torrey, who has written some of the best books on prayer ever published, said he could remember when he thought his prayer life would never get off the ground. He grew up in a Christian family where he was taught to pray as a child, but he said prayer was mostly a matter of rote and ritual—even after he entered the ministry. When he realized what real prayer meant, however—having an audience with God, actually coming into His presence and asking for and getting things from Him—his prayer life was transformed.

"Before that," he said, "prayer had been a mere duty, and sometimes a very irksome duty, but from that time on prayer has been not merely a duty but a privilege, one of the most highly esteemed privileges of life. Before that the thought that I had was, 'How much time must I spend in prayer?' The thought that now possesses me is, 'How much time may I spend in prayer without neglecting the other privileges and duties of life?'" Talking with God had become so special to him that he had to guard against it eating up his whole day![8]

The Lord's Prayer reminds us that God longs for His people to communicate with Him, to talk to Him in the same way we would speak with the most precious person in our life. We don't go home and say, "O, thou dear, most wonderful wife. How thou art blessing me this day!" If we pontificated and postured with our loved ones instead of communicating in a normal, natural way, our relationships would suffer greatly and probably wouldn't last long.

In the same vein, Jesus teaches us to approach God honestly, openly, and sincerely. We don't pray to impress people and there are no "special words" we must use before we're allowed into God's presence. Yet if we are to pray effectively, there are some key ideas to keep in mind. And that's what the Lord's Prayer is all about.

You are an omnipotent God! You indeed do have power! You can do anything! Nothing is too hard for You! There is no sickness that You cannot heal! There is no problem that You cannot solve! There is no challenge that You cannot meet! There is no financial deficit that You cannot overcome! There is no man who can overthrow Your purposes! There is no committee that can thwart Your work in the church of Jesus Christ. You are the all-powerful, magnificent, amazing, beyond comprehension, God! Lord, You are more than anything that I could say about You. There are no words to describe the greatness and glory and majesty of Jehovah-God!

THE NEXT GREAT REVIVAL?

If we get this remarkable prayer down deep into our hearts and minds, where it belongs, it cannot do less than change our lives. The truth is, at the moment we pray, we become subject to the most powerful force in the universe. Therefore if we ever get to the place where we can honestly and with integrity pray the Lord's Prayer in all that it means, we will see the next great revival sweep across America and around the world.

Never has revival been more needed than it is today. So let us dig into the Lord's Prayer. Let us see what we can learn from it and how we might be encouraged through it. And then let us take the last (and absolutely necessary) step.

Let us pray.

Chapter Five

PRAISE:

APPROACHING A HOLY FATHER

"Our Father who art in heaven, Hallowed be Thy name."

O ne of our greatest needs is to be loved by our father. This is true for all of us. Knowing that our father loves us gives us a stability and strength that simply changes everything. Dr. Ross Campbell, a specialist who works with children, tells this story:

After a recent trip out of town for a few days, I returned home to find my 5-year-old son, Dale, acting in a way that irritated me (and everyone else). He was doing all sorts of antics designed to aggravate the rest of the family, especially his 9-year-old brother, David. Dale needled his brother, pouted and made unreasonable demands. My first reaction was to send him to his room, perhaps put him to bed, perhaps spank him.

Then I stopped to think, *What does he need?* The answer came in an instant. He had not seen me in three days, and I had not really paid him much attention. He seemed to be asking the old, old question, "Do you love me?" Actually, Dale was asking, "Do you still love me after being gone so long and acting as though it didn't affect me?" Suddenly his behavior made sense. He desperately needed his daddy.

I took Dale to our bedroom, held him close and said nothing. That normally active fellow was still and quiet against me. He just sat there and absorbed all that intangible nurturing. Gradually, as his emotional tank was filled, he came to life. He began talking in his confident, easygoing, spontaneously happy way. After a short conversation about my trip, he jumped down and ran off. Where? To find his brother, of course. When I walked to the family room, they were playing contentedly together.

Almost every study I know indicates that every child is continually asking his parents, "Do you love me?" A child asks this emotional question mostly through his behavior, seldom verbally. The answer to this question is absolutely the most important thing in any child's life.[1]

The world changes when we know our father loves us. *We* change. And that is especially true when the father we're talking about is our Heavenly Father.

MORE THAN SERVANTS

The writers of the Old Testament had a much different concept of their relationship with God than we have today. When the scribes who copied the Old Testament Scriptures wrote the word for God, *Yahweh*, they would throw away their pen, never to use it again. They reasoned that once it had written the word *Yahweh*, the pen was disqualified to write anything else.

The men and women who worshiped God in Old Testament days had a great sense of fear and reverence for Him. (We would do well to learn some of that in our day of casual relating to the Almighty.) But the downside of their experience was a lack of personal intimacy with God. They had to approach Him through the Tabernacle, the Temple, and animal sacrifice. In the entire Old Testament, the word "father" is used to describe God only fourteen times, and in every instance it refers to God as the father of the Israelite nation. The people of Israel had a filial relationship to God, but it was national, not personal.

What a tremendous difference there is when you cross over the threshold into the New Testament! You can't get past Matthew before you're introduced to a whole new understanding of the Fatherhood of God. It is no longer national; it is now individual and personal. The word "Father" occurs seventeen times in the Sermon on the Mount alone. In the four Gospels, Jesus Christ refers to the Father more than seventy times.

What makes the difference? Galatians 4:4–7 explains: "But when the fulness of time came, God sent forth His Son, born of a woman, born under the Law, in order that He might redeem those who were under the Law, that we might receive *the adoption as sons*. And because you are sons, God has sent forth the Spirit of His Son into our hearts, crying 'Abba! Father!' Therefore you are no longer a slave, but a son; and if a son, then an heir through God" (emphasis added).

When Christ died on the cross, the veil between human beings and Almighty God was torn. A whole new way of approaching God was opened up to us. In the Old Testament we were servants; in the New Testament we are sons and daughters.

And how do we become His children? The only way to get into God's family is to be adopted. When we trust in Jesus Christ, who is God's only begotten Son, He alone gives us the privilege to be called a child of God. Only through Him can we lift our voices to heaven and say, "Our Father—*My Father*." The Apostle John says, "Behold, what manner of love the Father hath bestowed upon us, that we should be called the sons of God" (1 John 3:1, KJV). When I think about looking up into the face of a loving Heavenly Father who cares for me, and cares for me with more intense love than I can imagine, I can exclaim with John, "What manner of love is that!"

O Lord, You are my God and You have done wonderful things. How I praise You today for the wonderful things You have done in my life. As I meditate upon them this morning they are too wonderful for me to express. How I love my wife and my children. I can hardly speak of it without tears these days. Thank You so much for bringing Donna into my life and giving us these precious years together. In just a few months we will have been married for 32 years. In these years we have known so much joy and have seen You do so many wonderful things. It is true that we have known some pain. And at this very moment we are in the midst of one of the most difficult times we have ever known. . . but Lord, looking at all of those years, they have been mostly filled with joy and happiness and, yes, much success. We have traveled and ministered together and it has been a wonderful experience. Please, Lord, for Donna's sake as well as for mine, allow that this disease will be cured and I will be able to continue to love this woman and be her husband and friend.

When my own kids were growing up, it was understood that if they ever came to the church during the week, they could always get in to see me. It didn't matter when they came or who I was with. When my secretary rang my phone and told me that one of my children wanted to see me, I would excuse myself and go see him or her. While I couldn't do that with everybody—it would be mass chaos—I do that for my son; I do that for my daughter. A special bond exists between us. I'm their father! They can walk into my life any time they choose.

That's the way it is with our Father in Heaven. When you became a son or a daughter, when you were adopted into His family, He opened up for you through His Son's death on the cross a way of fellowship and relationship that makes it possible for you to bypass the temple and its animal sacrifices. You don't have to talk to God through a priest. You can go right into the presence of God Almighty and He will hear you. As the writer of Hebrews says, "We have confidence to enter the holy place by the blood of Jesus, by a new and living way which He inaugurated for us through the veil, that is, His flesh, and since we have a great priest over the house of God, let us draw near with a sincere heart in full assurance of faith" (Hebrews 10:19–22). Incredible!

I have recently entered into a relationship with AT&T in my own fathering responsibilities. We gave our son a calling card and we got an 800 number. I said to Daniel a few days ago, "Son, I know there's a time difference between where we are and where you are, but I want you to know that, no matter what, any time you need to call us, *any time*, you can do it. I really mean that."

Now, if I am like that as an earthly father with limited resources, what do you think the Father in heaven is like? He owns the cattle on a thousand hills and you don't need a phone card or 800 number to reach Him. He's waiting for you to walk into His presence…ANY TIME. And He won't send you a bill.

HE'S OUT OF THIS WORLD

By referring to God as His "Father," Jesus shows us the way of personal relationship between a son and his father. Yet He does not merely say, "Our Father"; He teaches us to pray to our Father *who art in heaven.*" Mentioning the place where God resides puts a different spin on it.

Jesus is careful to remind us that our Father is in heaven. The earth is His footstool and He is a God of majesty and might who is worthy of our worship. He is the glorious King, surrounded by the angelic host. He sits on the throne of majesty and at His right hand shines His Son, Jesus Christ. All the creatures of glory minister to the Lord. Think of all the pomp and circumstance you know in this world, multiply it by a thousand times a thousand, and you haven't touched anything of the glory and majesty of the Father who is in Heaven. As one author wrote a few years ago:

It seems in these days that God is enjoying keeping the astronomers on the edge of their seats with new glimpses of his power. In the fall of 1989, newspapers reported the discovery by two Harvard astronomers of a "Great Wall" of galaxies stretching hundreds of millions of light years across the known universe. The wall is supposedly some five hundred million light years long, two hundred million light years wide and fifteen million light years thick. In case your high school astronomy has grown fuzzy, a light year is a little less than six trillion (6,000,000,000,000) miles. This Great Wall consists of more than fifteen thousand galaxies, each with millions of stars, and was described as the "largest single coherent structure seen so far in nature."

I say "was described" because three months later in February 1990, God opened another little window for tiny man to marvel again, and the newspapers reported that astronomers have discovered more than a dozen evenly distributed clumps of galaxies stretching across vast expanses of the heavens, suggesting a structure to the universe that is so regular and immense that it defies current theories of cosmic origins. The newly found pattern of galactic matter dwarfs the extremely long sheet of galaxies, dubbed the "great wall" (now written without caps!), that was reported in November 1989 to be the largest structure in the universe. They now say the great wall is, in fact, merely one of the closest of these clumps, or regions, that contain very high concentrations of galaxies.

What is this universe but the lavish demonstration of the incredible, incomparable, unimaginable exuberance and wisdom and power and greatness of God! What a God he must be![2]

Yes, what a God He is! I believe that the church, in an effort to stress the intimacy God has given us with Himself through Christ, has moved too far away from reverence. I don't care for terms such as "The Big Dodger in the sky" or "The Man Upstairs." They don't reflect the true majesty and greatness of God. That kind of flippancy and extra-familiarity has no place in our conversation, for we serve an Almighty Heavenly Father of limitless power and glory and unimaginable awesomeness. God is uncommon. He is extraordinary. He is unearthly. He is separated from sinners. He is undefiled. He is holy. God is uniquely different and above all.

> *Lord, I know Who You are and I am so grateful that Your majesty is displayed in heaven and in the entire universe. I know that You see from Your vantage point all of the issues in my life and all of the matters of this world. You have a view that no one here has. You see the beginning of the parade and the end of it all at the same time. Lord, You are in heaven and I am on earth. I worship Your majesty this day. And yet at the same time, God, You are my Father. I cannot completely understand all of that, and I know that I never will. But to know that You are my Father is such a comfort to me. Lord, I want to be a father like You are to my children. You are gracious and kind. You remember that we are dust. You forgive and You encourage, and I want that to be true of me as well. Dear God, thank You for being my Father and for helping me to learn how to be a father as well!*

And yet He is our Father! On one hand, our Father is easy to approach because we are His beloved sons; on the other hand, He is the King of the universe, clothed in heavenly glory. I don't know about you, but that strips my gears! How do those two things go together?

When John F. Kennedy was President of the United States, *Life* magazine published photos of his children, John Jr. and Caroline, playing with their toys on the floor of the Oval Office. Those images captured the hearts of the American people like nothing before or since. Why? I think it's because it bridged a gap between two thoughts: Kennedy was the President of the United States, but he was also a father. He held ultimate political power in the Free World, but playing at his feet were two little kids who called him Daddy. I don't think your kids would have been allowed to do that. Nor mine. But his kids were. Why? He was their father. He was not only President of the United States; he was also their dad.

In the same way, God is both our Father and the Lord of glory. We can approach Him confidently in prayer because we are His dearly beloved children, but we must never forget that He is also the Sovereign of the universe. That is what we mean when we say, "Our Father, who art in heaven."

WHAT DOES "HALLOWED" MEAN?

Because God lives in heaven and possesses majesty and glory far beyond our ability to comprehend, He is to be "hallowed." When you hear the famous words, "Hallowed be Thy name," what comes to mind? Ivy covered buildings and long robes? A musty, dim church complete with mournful music and distant chants?

"Hallowed" is an archaic word not much used in conversation today. The word "hallow" comes from the Greek term *hagiazo* which means "to be holy." When we use it, we are saying, "Our Father in heaven, Your name is holy." We are setting God apart in our minds to be praised and adored.

John Calvin put it this way: "That God's name should be hallowed is to say that God should have His own honor of which He is so worthy, so that men should never think or speak of Him without the greatest veneration."[3] This may sound like a strictly "religious" activity, but it isn't. We do similar things, although on a smaller scale, in ordinary life. For example, consider the experience of author Donald McCullough when he and his wife were invited to hear the great tenor Luciano Pavarotti:

The concert exceeded our expectations. We were stunned by the master's music. In aria after aria he demonstrated remarkable talent—talent, surely, that set him apart from the thousands who had come to hear him. But that set-apartness was revealed in his generous giving; his uniqueness was shown in a gracious offering of himself. He held nothing back, it seemed. Every single note was filled with boundless passion and glorious beauty.

We *had* to respond: we jumped to our feet and we clapped, hooted, and whistled. We did not stop, not for a long time. Wave after wave of grateful applause was sent up to the platform, calling forth encore after encore.

In the midst of this mayhem of gratitude, when my hands were beginning to ache from the pounding, I thought to myself, *This is deeply satisfying, a profound joy.* It felt right to offer praise in response to such excellence, and this sense of appropriateness created a congruence in which my little world, at least for the moment, seemed perfectly ordered.

In a similar way, God's gracious self-giving in Jesus Christ calls for the response of faith, and faith's first expression will be the applause of praise. Worship—the word comes from middle English, meaning to ascribe worth—is both an instinctive response and an inexhaustible source of joy.[4]

Every time we think of what God has done and what He has given in Jesus Christ, we should lose ourselves in worship. Certainly, that is what our Lord had in mind when He taught His disciples to pray, "Our Father who art in heaven, *hallowed be Thy name*." In using these words, we should not think that God has degrees of holiness and that by coming to Him and hallowing His name we can somehow elevate His worth. God cannot be lifted any higher than He is, because already He is at the pinnacle of righteousness and holiness and greatness. But when we come into the presence of God with an attitude of worship and praise, deferring our own requests until we have paid Him the honor He is due, then we are hallowing His name. We are saying, "Father, we give you that which is rightly Yours. We acknowledge Your worth. We ascribe to You holiness. We glorify Your name."

Someone has well said that no religion ever rises higher than its concept of God. No church is ever greater than the value it places on the importance of personal and congregational worship. The Danish theologian Soren Kierkegaard said that "we have gotten confused about who's doing what in worship: we think of worshipers as an audience; pastors as entertainers; and God as the prompter. In fact, worshipers are performers; pastors are prompters; and God is the audience. When we gather for worship, whether with a handful in a storefront chapel or with thousands in St. Peter's Square, we perform a drama with different parts—speaking and singing and praying and giving money and baptizing and eating bread and drinking wine—all for the delight of God."[5]

Kierkegaard suggested a number of ways we "hallow" God's name: By speaking, singing, praying, giving money, baptizing, eating bread and drinking wine. How else can we hallow God's name? Let me suggest a few additional ways:

1. We hallow His name by rehearsing who He is

When we speak of hallowing someone's "name," we do not mean that we set apart the letters that make up the name. For instance, my name is spelled D-A-V-I-D. Those five letters by themselves don't mean anything. If you were to hallow my name, you wouldn't merely say, "'David'—now, that's quite a name." No, to hallow someone's name is to go beyond the name itself, beyond the letters, to set apart and magnify the one who stands behind the name. When Jesus instructed His followers to pray, "Hallowed be Thy name," He didn't specify which of God's names should be hallowed. Why not? He intended for us to honor the One who stands behind all the names, that at His name "every knee should bow."

We learn much about God from His names in the Bible. He is God the Father, He is Adonai, He is Yahweh, He is El Elyon. As we rehearse His names, we honor the One behind the names. The Old Testament uses eight compound names for God:

Yahweh Tsidkenu	The Lord our Righteousness
Yahweh M'kaddesh	The Lord who Sanctifies
Yahweh Shalom	The Lord who is our Peace
Yahweh Shammah	The Lord is there, he never leaves us
Yahweh Rophe	The Lord who Heals
Yahweh Jireh	The Lord who Provides
Yahweh Nissi	The Lord my Banner
Yahweh Rohi	The Lord who is my Shepherd

If we took just one of those names every day and focused on it, hallowing it, we would develop a much better understanding of who God is. For example, I have a sin problem (as you do), so I need Yahweh Tsidkenu, who is my righteousness. I have a problem being holy as God is holy, so I need Yahweh M'kaddesh, who is my sanctification. I sometimes have an anxiety problem and I need Yahweh Shalom, who is my peace. Once in a while, even though there are lots of people in my life, I am lonely. I need Yahweh Shammah, who is always there for me. I've gone through some sickness and I've desperately needed Yahweh Rophe, my Healer. I have needs in my family and I need Yahweh Jireh, the One who provides. Once in a while I'm not really sure who I am in the Kingdom of God, so I need Yahweh Nissi, who is my Banner. And I certainly couldn't handle my problems, my career, my decisions, without a Shepherd; how glad I am that I have Yahweh Rohi, my constant guide and companion!

As wonderful and strengthening as these names are, however, God's greatest revelation of Himself was the gift of His Son, Jesus. As the writer of Hebrews says,

God, after He spoke long ago to the fathers in the prophets in many portions and in many ways, in these last days has spoken to us in His Son, whom He appointed heir of all things, through whom also He made the world. And He is the radiance of His glory and the exact representation of His nature, and upholds all things by the word of His power (Hebrews 1:1–3).

The New Testament is full of descriptive names for Jesus: the Bread of Life; the Living Water; the Way, the Truth, and the Life; the Resurrection; the Good Shepherd; the True Vine; the Bright Morning Star; the Lamb of God; the Gate; and so many more. When we rehearse the names of God and Christ, we don't just memorize a list; we get little pictures of who He is. And when we praise the part of God's nature that is closest to the greatest need we have at the moment, we hallow His name and grow in our appreciation of His character.

2. We hallow His name by relinquishing control of our lives

Martin Luther once said that "God's name is hallowed among us when both our doctrines and our living are Christian."[6] In other words, if He is the Sovereign of the universe that we say He is through our praise and worship, then we must honor our Father by *doing* what He says.

The psalmist prayed, "Let the words of my mouth and the meditation of my heart be acceptable in Thy sight, O Lord, my rock and my Redeemer" (Psalm 19:14). That's what it means to hallow God's name. It means saying, "Lord, this day of my life is yours. Let me live in such a way, do my business dealings in such a way, interact with my family and my neighbors in such a way, that when people see me they say, 'I know what family he comes from. He belongs to the Father.'"

Can we live that way? *No we can't!* We cannot live in such a way in our own strength. Not for a day, not for an hour, not for a minute. But by the Holy Spirit's power we can relinquish control to God and allow Him to live through us. When people see that we are unique, that our lives are different, that there is a quality about us that goes beyond the natural, *then* the Father's name is glorified.

3. We hallow His name by recognizing His presence in our lives

When we are constantly aware of the presence of God, when we live every moment in light of the fact that He is our God, we hallow His name.

The psalmist wrote, "I have set the LORD always before me" (Psalm 16:8, NIV). We need to acknowledge God's presence at the *outset* of our prayers, rather than waiting until we're through our list of requests to add, "Oh, by the way, God, You're pretty great, too." God wants us always to acknowledge Him as our Father in heaven, and then to spend some time in praise and worship.

SEVEN BENEFITS OF PRAISE

When we begin our prayers as the Lord instructed us, not only are we approaching God in a way that pleases Him, but we are achieving for ourselves at least seven amazing benefits:

1. Worship enhances our appreciation and love for God

Did you know that by speaking words of praise (even if we don't feel like it), those words begin to explode within us so that we see God more clearly? When we diligently focus our attention on some aspect of the greatness of God, our appreciation and love for God grow enormously.

2. Worship expands our vision

If we don't worship, our vision shrinks. When we think of life in terms of what we can do, we lose sight of what our gifts and abilities could be if we put them in the hands of God. When we worship and praise God, our vision is expanded and we begin to look at life not in terms of what we can do, but of what God can do through us! Our perspective shifts. It's like staring at one of those two dimensional posters that suddenly leaps out at us in three dimensions. Suddenly we begin to see things we never saw before. Everything changes when God is in the picture.

3. Worship eclipses our fears

I have visited fear often in recent days. But when I worship God, I soon forget those things that gnaw at me. I begin to realize that I'm a child of the King; I am in His hands. I was reminded of this recently when I reread the journal I had been keeping during my battle against cancer. One entry says, "During these special days in my life, I am learning that You are able to do anything. I believe that Your hand has been in each detail of this illness and today of all days I want to give You praise for Your healing power. When the call came from Dr. Saven that the pathology report had turned out so positive, I felt as if a ton had been lifted off my back. Lord, I know that this is not over yet, but this gives us great hope and it seems as if we have turned the corner. I do not know why we have had so many turns and ups and downs. I have been on the mountain one day and in the valley the next. But You, O Lord, have been there with me in each situation. 'I will praise You with my whole heart; before the gods I will sing praises to You. I will worship toward Your holy temple, and praise Your name for Your lovingkindness and Your truth; for You have magnified Your word above all Your name' (Psalm 138:1–2, NKJV)."

4. Worship energizes our work

One of the great prayer warriors, Andrew Murray, wrote about having so much to do one day that he had to add an extra hour of prayer. When I follow his example, putting God first by worshiping Him, my work gets done better. The people I was going to call, call me. I bump into people I need to talk to in a restaurant. In two minutes I take care of something that would have normally taken me thirty minutes. When I hallow His name, my work gets done—not all of it, but most of it. When I put God first, God takes care of me and energizes me to do what really needs to be done.

5. *Worship refreshes our spirit*

When I go to bed with challenges or problems on my mind, sometimes I wake up with a heaviness. I might not even know why I'm feeling burdened. I've discovered that if I get into the presence of God and begin to worship Him, not even talking to Him about my heaviness, little by little the spirit of heaviness is exchanged for a garment of praise. My spirit is refreshed. That's what worship does.

6. *Worship exhausts our enemy*

Satan trembles when he sees the least of God's children on their knees. He doesn't like praise; it makes him incredibly uncomfortable. Whatever he wants to do, he has to work ten times harder to do it when God's people are praying. Wouldn't you like to see him exhausted and worn out by your prayers and praise? Worship, hallowing the name of the Lord, is a great weapon for spiritual warfare. I love to worship not only because of what I know it means to God, but because it's a powerful way to combat the Evil One.

7. *Worship prepares us for heaven*

One of the great presidents of Wheaton College was Raymond Edman. He felt passionately about reverence before God and he used to teach his students that worship was a serious matter. One day he was illustrating a talk on worship by describing a visit to Haile Selassie, the former emperor of Ethiopia. Edman described the preliminary briefings, the protocol he had to follow, and the way he bowed with respect as he entered the presence of the king. "In the same way," he said, "we must prepare ourselves to meet God." At that very moment Dr. Edman slumped onto the pulpit, fell to the floor, and entered the presence of the King of kings.[7] People have said that he had the easiest transition to heaven of anybody they've ever known, that he lived so much of his life in the presence of God down here that he simply changed venues.

Does that strike a spark in your heart? Do you say, "God, help me to worship You, help me to live in Your presence here, so that when the time comes for me to change venues, it won't be a major transition"? That is the honest cry of my own heart. I hope it is yours as well.

AN INTIMATE CONVERSATION WITH JESUS

A former Catholic priest named Brennan Manning received a phone call one day from someone he had never met, asking if he would go to the hospital to visit a dying man. He went. The man lay in bed, a chair pulled up next to him. "I'm going to die," he said. "I know that. But before I do, I've got to ask you a question. Some years ago I was struggling with my prayer life and someone told me that it would help me a lot if I could remember that prayer is a conversation, an intimate conversation with God. They suggested I set a chair out where I pray and imagine that I was having a conversation with the Lord Jesus, and the Lord Jesus was in that chair. I've been doing that. Sometimes I pray for over an hour, remembering that Jesus is there. Is that all right?"

> *Tonight I sat on the floor and just talked to You as a friend talks to a friend. I sensed Your presence and I am so thankful. Lord, I love you—I praise Your name—You are a great God—You are my God! Amen!*

Father Manning told him, "It's not only all right, but I think it delights the heart of God that your prayer is an intimate conversation with Him."

A few days later Manning got a call from the daughter of the man, saying that her father had died and they'd found his body in a strange position. "When we walked into his hospital room, his head was leaning on a chair by his bed."[8]

That man had come to understand what the Lord's Prayer is all about. It means coming to a Heavenly Father whose residence is in heaven and whose name is holy and infinitely praiseworthy. It means exulting in an eternal relationship with the Creator of the universe who has promised to clothe us with a divine holiness that outshines a thousand suns. And it means laying our head on His lap and falling asleep there, content, unafraid, and utterly happy. For eternity!

Chapter Six

PRIORITIES:

ALIGNING OUR WILL WITH GOD'S

"Thy kingdom come; Thy will be done on earth as it is in heaven."

I frequently cringe at the advice doled out in the nation's newspapers by Ann Landers, but she also gets things right once in awhile. Consider the following exchange:

Dear Ann Landers: I hesitate to write to you about this because the questions sound stupid, but I need some advice.

I'm a 38-year-old man, happily married for eight years, and have two young daughters. I've been at my job since 1974, the year after I graduated from college. It's not the biggest business of its kind, but it's been good to me and I've become the proverbial big fish in a small pond.

The problem is this: Over the years I've run into several college buddies, and most of them have done much better financially and career-wise than I have. When I compare my accomplishments to theirs, I always come up short and wind up feeling inferior and depressed.

I'll be the first to admit that I haven't been as aggressive as some of the guys I used to run around with. I should tell you that I've turned down a couple of job offers with better pay in order to stay in this city with my family, because we like it here. I also confess that I lack self-confidence.

I've never attended a college reunion because I feel like a failure around these guys. I haven't spoken to the ones who were my closest friends in 15 years because I'm ashamed to tell them I'm still at my first job. To be perfectly honest, an 8-year-old car doesn't quite cut the same swath as a new BMW or Ford Taurus.

How can I prove to my old college friends that I'm not a loser? What can I do to show them I'm OK, too?

Class of '73

Dear Class of '73: Since when does having a new BMW or Ford Taurus and a sizable bank account make a man a big success? You need to sit back and take a good look at your priorities, mister.

It sounds as if that "small pond" suits you just fine, so stop looking longingly at the ocean where life might be much more hazardous and not nearly as rewarding. All that glitters is not gold. The guys you are envying may be envying you.[1]

You nailed it, Ann!

The columnist couldn't have been more on target with her counsel. Especially when she said, "take a good look at your priorities, mister." When we get ourselves into trouble, it's usually because we *haven't* been taking a good look at our priorities. On the other hand, if our priorities are in order, then our life usually follows suit.

But how do we order our priorities? How do we know what items ought to take priority and which ought to slide? I can think of no better place to discover proper priorities than in the prayer Jesus taught His disciples. When the Lord taught His followers to pray, "Thy kingdom come. Thy will be done on earth as it is in heaven," He was teaching them how to pray God's priorities.

Learning how to pray God's priorities into my life has been one of the most exciting things I have ever learned. When I discover and do God's will for my life, I enjoy adventure, excitement, and every full-orbed blessing He wants for me.

THE REIGN OF CHRIST

What does it mean to pray, "Thy kingdom come"?

The Bible says that if you are a Christian, the kingdom of God is within you; the King has come to live within your heart (see Luke 17:21). When you pray "Thy kingdom come," you are saying, "God, You are the King. You live in my heart. And I want Your kingdom principles and purposes to be lived out within me, as You reign within me. I know the manifest, visible kingdom isn't here on this earth yet, but there can be a little touch of the kingdom within me as I walk with You and talk with You and live for You each day." God has called us to live as if the King were already in residence on this earth, because He does reside in our hearts.

Not only is the kingdom within us, but there is a glimmer of the kingdom around us in our brothers and sisters in Christ. The church is not the kingdom of God, but there is more of the kingdom of God in the church than there is in the world! When God's people come together, a little bit of the kingdom of God is manifested. The church has the opportunity to live out kingdom principles in the midst of a decadent and dying world. Regardless of the messy state of affairs around us, God isn't off duty. He hasn't gone to sleep. His kingdom is still alive and well and being manifested in the lives of His people on earth.

There is also a kingdom yet before us. A day is coming, perhaps very soon, when the trumpet will sound and the Lord will descend and all who have put their trust in Him will be raptured into His presence. Immediately after that, according to the Gospel of Matthew, there will be a period of unprecedented tribulation that will last for seven years. At its conclusion, Jesus Christ will come back from heaven with His saints and angels and will set up His kingdom on this earth for a thousand years.

> *Lord, I am not exactly sure what this might mean, but I do know that Your kingdom will come in its fulness some day, and I also know that You are at work establishing Your kingdom in the hearts of Your children even at this time! I cannot pray enough for the importance of the kingdom of God in this land as we stand in the face of this election. Lord, I want to ask that You would do something so great that it would shock the American people. I pray that You will have Your way in this election. Lord, I want to trust You that our country can be saved from the oblivion of moral disaster, but I ask that You will show Your power in these next few days that when the election is over, however it turns out, we will be able to see Your hand in it all! Help me to deal rightly with the political issue on Sunday, and please, Lord, give me wisdom as I try to sort out what I am to be doing in the kingdom issues of this day.*

What will it be like when the King rules the earth? The Old Testament describes it this way: "They will hammer their swords into plowshares, and their spears into pruning hooks. Nation will not lift up sword against nation, and never again will they learn war" (Isaiah 2:4, also Micah 4:3). People will abandon everything military and become agricultural once more. The lion and the wolf will lie down with the lamb and children will play by the hole of the cobra (Isaiah 11:8).

This is why Jesus taught His disciples it was legitimate to pray, "O God, may Your kingdom come! Let Your kingdom come within me; let the King rule in my life. Let the kingdom come around me; let kingdom principles be manifest among God's people. But most of all, Lord, hasten the day of Your coming, when everything is going to be made right."

But let me warn you: If you ever start to pray that prayer sincerely, *get ready for war*.

There are two kingdoms, and the kingdom that's in operation right now doesn't like the kingdom that's coming. God's kingdom is not of this world. His kingdom is manifest *in* this world, but it's not *of* this world. Satan is running most things right now. He is the prince of the power of the air and God has given him permission, for a while, to have his way. He's on a leash, but it's a rather long leash—long enough to let him touch you and me. When you start to live out kingdom principles, you'll get the attention of the evil one. He doesn't like it when you do what Matthew 6:33 says: "But seek first His [God's] kingdom and His right-eousness; and all these things shall be added to you." When you start living like a kingdom child, you'll have some struggles.

Don't let that stop you, however—you also have the King! It is the King who promises, "He who overcomes, I will grant to him to sit down with Me on My throne, as I also overcame and sat down with My Father on His throne" (Revelation 3:21). As Andrew Murray wrote, "The children of the Father are here in the enemy's territory, where the kingdom, which is in heaven, is not yet fully manifested. What is more natural than that when they learn to hallow the Father-name, they should long and cry with deep enthusiasm: 'Thy kingdom come.'"[2]

THE RULE OF CHRIST

As necessary as it is, the Lord taught us that praying "Thy kingdom come" is not enough. We must add, "Thy will be done on earth as it is in heaven." In other words, first we are to pray God's priorities regarding the reign of Christ; then we are to pray God's priorities regarding the rule of Christ.

Many folks who grew up in the church don't want to pray "Thy will be done" because they're afraid the will of God means Africa, India, New

Guinea—missionary service somewhere that will require total poverty and the end of all relationships they have known. They're afraid that as soon as they say, "God, You can do whatever You want with me," He's going to pack them off to the worst place in the world, some pit where they never wanted to go in the first place.

Wait a minute! Is He that kind of a Father? Do we think God is up in heaven just waiting for us to say "yes" to Him so He can do the worst thing in the world to us? I don't think so. That's one of the enemy's lies. He wants us to believe that if we ask for God's will in our lives, we're signing up for a journey of no return.

Richard Baxter, a great Puritan thinker and writer, well understood the real truth. He used to write these words whenever he was asked to sign one of his books: "Lord, what Thou wilt, where Thou wilt, and when Thou wilt." In the old Puritan manner of speaking he was saying, "Lord, whatever you want, wherever you want it, and whenever you want it, that's what I want."[3] That is how to pray the rule of Christ into our lives every day. And it's a struggle! At least, it is for me.

I'm highly task oriented; I want to get things done. It's easy for me to rush into the day with my to-do list, oblivious to the fact that the Lord might want to rearrange my priorities. He might want to drop some things at the top of my list down to the middle and push some things at the bottom up to the top.

One writer has said, "God expects us to be orderly. He expects us to manage our time, to discipline ourselves, to prepare well-planned programs. But if we could learn to pray first and plan afterward, how different would be our homes, our churches, our Christian clubs, our Bible studies, whatever we are doing for Christ. Maybe, just maybe, we are planning in one direction and God's will is in another direction. God might say, 'Hold everything! Turn around and go this way. This is My will for you, not that way.'"[4]

> *I am writing these prayers to You because my mind so easily wanders from the thought process when I pray in another way. I want to be working things out with You in my prayer time, and I believe that I am learning how to do that, at least in some measure. I realize more than ever before that this time is more important than sermon preparation, or even than the preaching of a sermon. If I do not work things out with You, I am doomed to failure and frustration and fatigue!*

It's taken me awhile to learn this. I started out in the ministry thirty years ago at a church in Fort Wayne, Indiana. And I was *focused*. Man, was I focused! I wasn't necessarily aiming to be a spiritual success; I just didn't want to be a miserable failure. Everybody knew Jeremiah went to Fort Wayne to start a church. I was knocking on doors every spare moment, all day Saturday and Sunday, in the afternoon, at night. I was gone all the time. I was doing the work of God! What could be better?

But at that time, my wife Donna and I had two little children. Jan was a newborn and David was just thirteen months older. While Donna was at home with our kids, I was out on my white horse, winning people to Jesus and building the church. When I came home Donna would say to me, "Are you going to be gone again tonight?" I wanted to say (but I never did), "Woman, I'm God's man in this place. If I don't do this, it's not going to get done!" So I'd go out and knock on some more doors, only to come home to the hurt look on my dear wife's face. I thought I was doing God's will; but really, I was doing David's will. I just didn't want to fail.

One day, Donna sat me down in the kitchen and said, "Honey, I just want to tell you I am never going to ask you again, 'Are you going to be gone tonight?' I've been thinking and praying about this, and the fact is, you are the priest in this family and one day you're going to have to stand before God and give account of how you led us. If you believe God wants you to lead us by being gone all the time, then I'm not going to argue with you. This is all in your lap now. You are responsible."

Gotcha!

That was a turning point in my life. I realized there are no ultimate conflicts in God's perfect will. He doesn't call a man to be both a father and a pastor in such a way that those two roles constantly war against each other. I began to pray God's priorities back into my life. Soon they became crystal clear to me.

First, I am a person with a responsibility before God. Then I am a partner with a responsibility to my wife. Then I am a parent with a responsibility to my kids. Last, I am a pastor with a responsibility to my congregation.

Sometimes attending to my family's needs keeps me from doing things at church that I might really want to do. For instance, one afternoon I was getting ready to leave my office to see my son David play basketball. I don't miss basketball or football games; I don't miss any of my children's games if I can possibly be there. As I was heading out the door, a call came from my assistant downstairs: A guy had just walked in, totally frantic, saying he had to see Pastor Jeremiah *right now!* I replied that I couldn't see him; I had to be at the game in fifteen minutes.

"What do I tell him?" she asked.

"Glenda," I replied, "there are five other pastors up here. Let him talk to one of them. I'm gone to the ball game."

I took the elevator downstairs and had to walk through the lobby. This guy was there, and he was bold. He walked up to me, got right in my face, and yelled, "Where are you going!?"

"I'm going to watch my son play basketball."

He went ballistic. "You're *what?* You're going *where?* Here my family's coming unglued, and you're going to a *ball game?*"

Without thinking, I answered him matter-of-factly: "Sir, there are five guys upstairs who can help you, probably better than I can. But my son has only one dad, so I'm gone."

That's how ruthless we sometimes have to be to keep our priorities in the will of God. It's hard when we have allowed other people to direct our life. But I know God doesn't want that; *He* wants to control my life. And failure to discover and do the Lord's will is more than sin; it can be disastrous in the here and now. The following story broke my heart and I'm sad to say it's not all that unusual:

There was a little boy who kept asking his father, "Dad, will you come out to the back yard and help me build a treehouse?" And this boy's father, always with the best intentions, said, "Sure, son—but later, OK? I'm really busy right now, but we'll build that treehouse real soon." Many times this boy asked his father that question; the answer was always the same.

But one day, this little boy was hit by a car. As he lay dying in the hospital, one of the last things he said to his dad was, "Well, Dad, I guess we'll never get to build that treehouse."

This is a true story. I officiated at that little boy's funeral. I talked with his grieving father. And I know that there are two lessons that each of us—myself included—can learn from this story.

First, if you're a parent (and especially if you're a father) you need to recognize that nothing—not the pressure of business nor your community commitments nor your church commitments—*nothing* is more urgent and more important than the relationship you are building with that child. Don't neglect it.

Second, understand that you have a *Heavenly Father* who is *always* available, always ready to take the time to build a relationship with you. I urge you to take time for those all-important relationships between you and your children—and you and your God.[5]

What a reminder of right priorities this story gives us! Like everyone else, I sometimes fail, but what a joy it is to pray to God the way Jesus showed me: "Lord, *Thy* will be done." When we pray according to the will of God, we get on the same wavelength as God. And as we pray, little by little, God takes all the things that are out of sync in our life and puts them in sync until we can take a deep breath and say, "Oh, yes, that's the way it's supposed to be!"

Oswald Chambers has written, "It is not so true that prayer changes things as that prayer changes me, and then I change things; consequently we must not ask God to do what He has created us to do. For instance, Jesus Christ is not a social reformer; He came to alter us first, and if there is any social reform to be done on earth, we must do it."[6] Chambers believed that "Prayer alters a man on the inside, alters his mind and his attitude to things. The point of praying is not that we get things from God, but that we learn by prayer to detect the difference between God's order and God's permissive will. God's order is—no pain, no sickness, no devil, no war, no sin; His permissive will is all these things. What a man needs to do is to get hold of God's order in the kingdom on the inside, and then he will begin to see how to handle the riddle of the universe on the outside."[7]

Do you need to discover how to handle the riddle of the universe? Then you will make it a priority to learn to pray, "Thy will be done."

AS IT IS IN HEAVEN

And how is God's will done in heaven? How do the angels do the will of God? Do they say, "Well, Lord, I know that's important—but I'd rather do it tomorrow"? Do they reply, "Lord, I know you wanted Michael to do that, but I think that's more suited to Gabriel's skill set. Why don't you get Gabriel to do it?"

The angels do the will of God immediately, unreservedly, unconditionally, joyfully. They do it because they have just been commanded by the greatest Power in the universe, a Power they would never defy. When He commands, they obey.

What would happen if we responded to the will of God as do the angels in heaven? How much energy would we save if we said, "All right, Lord, I don't understand it, it doesn't make a lot of sense to me, I can't figure it all out—but if this is Your will, I'm going to do it. I don't want to get out of sync with You"?

One author has written, "In heaven God's will is done, and the Master teaches the child to ask that His will may be done on earth just as in heaven: in the spirit of adoring submission and ready obedience... where faith has accepted the Father's love, obedience accepts the Father's will."[8]

More than a century ago Dwight L. Moody, founder of the Moody Bible Institute, was sitting in a hay mow in Ireland, listening to a preacher named Henry Barley. "The world has yet to see what God can do with and for and through a man who is fully and wholly consecrated to Him," Barley declared. Moody later said that something turned on in his heart that day. Five and a half years later he was sitting way up in the balcony of Charles Spurgeon's church in London, England, and the words of Henry Barley came back to him: "...with a man, for a man, through a man fully and wholly consecrated to God." In the balcony of that great church, Moody bowed his head and said, "Lord, if there were ever a man who would commit himself to such a way, here's one." He went out from that place to set the world on fire.[9]

Have you ever thought about what God could do in you if you were fully, totally, completely, unreservedly, immediately available to do whatever He asked you to do? You may be thinking, *Well, I've been trying to do that. But it doesn't look like God's doing anything in response. It doesn't look like God's even hearing my prayers.* You know, the King doesn't always have to tell His subjects every detail of what He's up to. But God is always up to something. You've got to trust Him. I was reminded of this the other day when I saw the following true story reported by a worker with the Overseas Missionary Fellowship:

> While serving at a small field hospital in Africa, I traveled every two weeks by bicycle through the jungle to a nearby city for supplies. This requires camping overnight halfway. On one of these trips, I saw two men fighting in the city. One was seriously hurt so I treated him and witnessed to him about the Lord Jesus Christ. I then returned home without incident.
>
> Upon arriving in the city several weeks later, I was approached by the man I had treated earlier. He told me he had known that I carried money and medicine. He said, "Some friends and I followed you into the jungle, knowing you would camp overnight. We waited for you to go to sleep and planned to kill you and take your money and drugs. Just as we were about to move into your campsite, we saw that you were surrounded by 26 armed guards."
>
> I laughed at this and said, "I was certainly all alone out in the jungle campsite."
>
> The young man pressed the point, "No sir, I was not the only one to see the guards. My five friends also saw them, and we all counted them. It was because of those guards that we were afraid and left you alone."
>
> At this point of my church presentation in Michigan, one of the men in the church stood up and interrupted me. He asked, "Can you tell me the exact date when this happened?"
>
> I thought for awhile and recalled the date.
>
> The man in the congregation then gave his side of the story. He stated, "On that night in Africa it was day here. I was preparing to play golf. As I put my bags in the car, I felt the Lord leading me to pray for you. In fact, the urging was so great that I

called the men of this church together to pray for you. Will all of those men who met to pray please stand?"

The men who had met that day to pray together stood—there were 26 of them![10]

What might have happened to that medical worker had the man back in the United States chosen to ignore God's call to pray? What might have occurred had he said, "Well, Lord, this just doesn't make any sense to me. I'm getting ready to golf, anyway. I'll pray when I get home. In the meanwhile, why don't you teach that man to pray for his own needs?"

This dramatic story reminds us of the power of praying in God's will. But what if the missionary had no such story to report? What if the golfer never heard about what his prayers had accomplished? To be honest, that's the way it is with most of our prayers. We may feel an urging to pray for someone, but seldom do we hear of any "miraculous" answers in response. We may pray for something or someone for years and never see anything happen. Does that mean that nothing is happening, that we should give up and use our energy on something more productive?

No. God is at work in response to our prayers, whether we see something happening or not. If we are truly praying, "Thy will be done," forces are at work beyond our comprehension—and often, beyond our vision. But they are working just the same.

HOW DO WE DISCOVER HIS WILL?

It's one thing to be committed to doing God's will; but how do we find it in the first place? How can we know what God's will is for us in particular circumstances?

George Mueller said, "I never remember...a period...that I ever sincerely and patiently sought to know the will of God by the teaching of the Holy Ghost, through the instrumentality of the Word of God, but I have been always directed rightly. But if honesty of heart and uprightness before God were lacking, or if I did not patiently wait upon God for instruction, or if I preferred the counsel of my fellow men to the declarations of the Word of the living God, I made great mistakes."[11]

Mueller followed six basic steps to discern God's heart:

1. I seek at the beginning to get my heart into such a state that it has no will of its own in regard to a given matter. Nine-tenths of the trouble with people generally is just here. Nine-tenths of the difficulties are overcome when our hearts are ready to do the knowledge of what His will is.

2. Having done this, I do not leave the result to feeling or simple impression. If so, I make myself liable to great delusions.

3. I seek the Will of the Spirit of God through, or in connection with, the Word of God. The Spirit and the Word must be combined. If I look to the Spirit alone without the Word, I lay myself open to great delusions also. If the Holy Ghost guides us at all, He will do it according to the Scriptures and never contrary to them.

4. Next I take into account providential circumstances. These often plainly indicate God's Will in connection with His Word and Spirit.

5. I ask God in prayer to reveal His will to me aright.

6. Thus, (1) through prayer to God, (2) the study of the Word, and (3) reflection, I come to deliberate judgment according to the best of my ability and knowledge, and if my mind is thus at peace, and continues so after two of three more petitions, I proceed accordingly."[12]

The author of the bestselling *Experiencing God* boils it down to this:
- Agree with God that you will follow Him one day at a time.
- Agree to follow Him even when He does not spell out all the details.

• Agree that you will let Him be your Way.[13]

In other words, find out where the Master is—then that is where you need to be. Find out what the Master is doing—then that is what you need to be doing. Jesus says, "If anyone serves Me, let him follow Me; and where I am, there shall My servant also be; if anyone serves Me, the Father will honor him" (John 12:26).

So does this mean that if we find God's will and do it, everything will always come up roses? Hardly. His will may involve some difficult and trying times. But regardless of how hot the oven might get, the center of God's will is always the safest place for any of us to be. As one writer has pointed out,

> The disciples were in a boat in a storm. Jesus was asleep in the back of the boat. If you had gone to those disciples in the middle of that storm, and said, to them, "What is the truth of this situation?" what would they have said? "We perish!" Was that the truth? No, the Truth was asleep in the back of the boat. Truth is a person. In just a moment Truth Himself would stand up, and He would still the storm. Then they knew the Truth of their circumstance. Truth is a person who is always present in your life. You cannot know the truth of your circumstance until you have heard from God. He is the Truth! And the Truth is present and active in your life.[14]

As this is the last day of the year 1994, I want to express my deep love and appreciation to you, Lord, for Your guidance and direction in my life during the past 365 days. In spite of the bend in the road, You have been so gracious to me and to my family. For one thing, I sure did discover how many people loved us and were praying for us at this time. Thank You for the safety of every one of my children and family members, as we have all traveled many miles this past year.

THE AMAZING RESULTS OF DOING GOD'S WILL

When our priorities line up with God's priorities, it's amazing what results. Remember Ann Landers's column at the beginning of this chapter? A young father worried that his choice to put his family before his job would cause his college buddies to ridicule him. A few weeks after that column appeared, Ann received several replies. Let me reproduce just two of them:

> My advice to people who think the fast track is the way to go: Forget it. I chose that route and it hasn't made me or my family happy. The more money I make, the more we spend. It's a vicious circle. I'm saddled with a huge mortgage and we do a lot of meaningless stuff to keep up appearances. If I had it to do over again, I'd do it differently.
>
> **Schaumburg, Ill.**

> Please print this response to "Class of '73" who felt inadequate when he compared his success to that of his college classmates.
>
> My husband is probably one of the guys he admires. We have moved six times in 10 years, always for a better paying, more prestigious job. Each move requires establishing new friendships and becoming part of the community. I dream of staying in one place long enough for my children to develop ongoing relationships, but I know it will never happen.
>
> We drive the BMW that "Class of '73" admires as a status symbol. Actually, we have two. Sounds wonderful? Not really. What I wouldn't give for a husband who is satisfied with his job, his salary and the city we live in. My husband's lucky that I am committed to keeping our family life strong and loving. Some

days I feel like throwing in the towel. I envy your wife, Mr. "Class of '73."

K.B., Anytown, U.S.A.[15]

I never thought Ann Landers would be an evangelist for "Thy will be done," but in this instance, she was. Getting our priorities aligned with the priorities of God leads to more fulfillment and more joy, not less. As Henry Blackaby has written, "I think God is crying out and shouting to us, 'Don't just do something, stand there! Enter into a love relationship with Me. Get to know Me. Adjust your life to Me. Let Me love you and reveal Myself to you as I work through you.' A time will come when the doing will be called for, but we cannot skip the relationship. The relationship with God must come first."[16]

And that relationship is immeasurably strengthened and deepened when we learn to pray, as Jesus taught us, "Thy kingdom come. Thy will be done on earth, as it is in heaven." It's a powerful prayer that brings powerful results because it's directed to an all-powerful God.

Chapter Seven

PROVISION:

ASKING FOR WHAT WE NEED

"Give us this day our daily bread."

I t has been said that this magnificent prayer starts and ends on the highest of mountain peaks. It begins with our Father in heaven glorified and finishes with His kingdom and glory. In between, however, we take a journey into the valley where all of us live…into the lowland of human need. We start the prayer with God, we end the prayer with God. But between those two majestic summits are the concerns we deal with every day—our need for right priorities, for protection, for provision.

This is what Jesus has in mind when He instructs us to pray for our "daily bread." By this point in His prayer, our Lord says it's time to ask. We have praised God for who He is and oriented ourselves to His kingdom rule. Now He tells us to ask. What exactly does He mean?

ENCOURAGEMENT TO DEPEND UPON GOD

By instructing us to pray for our daily bread, the Lord reminds us that, regardless of our place in life, we all depend totally upon God for the daily supply of our material needs. Of course, we depend upon Him for everything—for breath, for life, for companionship, for emotional support, for spiritual guidance, for vision, for hope—but here He focuses primarily on our physical needs. At other times He would say things such as, "Man shall not live on bread alone" (Matthew 4:4) or "I am the bread of life" (John 6:35); but here in this great prayer He has in mind the physical necessities of life, represented by bread.

> It was almost three months to this day that I discovered that I had cancer. On September 26th at the Scripps Hospital, the mass near my spleen was discovered. Today I returned to the Scripps Clinic to have another CT Scan in order to determine if the chemotherapy was working effectively. I cannot convey in words the mixed emotions that I felt as I once again submitted to this test. I knew that I would not know anything about the results until my appointment with Dr. Saven on Tuesday. Once again, I had to trust You, Lord, that You are in charge of all of this. Thank You for being there with me and assuring me of Your love for me at this time.

GOD THE SUSTAINER

Psalm 104 is a magnificent hymn that praises God for His sustaining work throughout the earth. The psalmist says God

> sends forth springs in the valleys; they flow between the mountains; they give drink to every beast of the field; the wild donkeys quench their thirst. Beside them the birds of the heavens dwell; they lift up their voices among the branches. He waters the mountains from His upper chambers; the earth is satisfied with the fruit of His works. He causes the grass to grow for the cattle, and vegetation for the labor of man, so that he may bring forth food from the earth, and wine which makes man's heart glad, so that he may make his face glisten with oil, and food which sustains man's heart. The trees of the LORD drink their fill, the cedars of Lebanon which He planted, where the birds build their nests, and the stork, whose home is the fir trees. The high

mountains are for the wild goats; the cliffs are a refuge for the rock badgers…the young lions roar after their prey, and seek their food from God. (Psalm 104:10–21)

All of these creatures—donkeys, cattle, birds, goats, rock badgers, lions, humankind—depend upon God every moment of their lives. As the psalmist says, "They all wait for Thee, to give them their food in due season. Thou dost give to them, they gather it up; Thou dost open Thy hand, they are satisfied with good. Thou dost hide Thy face, they are dismayed; Thou dost take away their spirit, they expire, and return to their dust" (Psalm 104:27–29).

If for one minute God closes His hand or for one instant doesn't provide, we are all in trouble. God is the One who ultimately feeds the mouths of all mankind. It doesn't matter which mouth it is or where the mouth is located; if it gets filled, God is the One who put the food there.

IS GOD DOING A LOUSY JOB?

Someone might say, "But doesn't this imply that God is doing a pretty lousy job in half the world? How do you explain the famines that take thousands of lives every year? How do you explain the staring eyes and bloated bellies that newscasts regularly bring into our homes? If God is responsible for feeding the birds of the air and the beasts of the field and the men and women of the earth, then why do so many die?"

A full answer to that important and legitimate question lies beyond the scope of this chapter. The short answer, however, has two parts:

1. We live in a fallen world in which starvation and disease and death is part of the barren landscape. When Paul writes that "the creation was subjected to futility, not of its own will," that it is a slave to "corruption" and that "the whole creation groans and suffers the pains of childbirth together until now" (Romans 8:20, 21, 22), he means that catastrophes like food shortages and war and tornadoes and earthquakes will afflict

humankind until the day God renews the world and rids it of sin. That day is yet future. Jesus Himself had predicted "in various places there will be famines" (Matthew 24:7). He also reminded us in John 12:8, "the poor you always have with you," and He knew it was the poor who usually found their stomachs empty. That is why He also said, "Blessed are you who are poor, for yours is the kingdom of God. Blessed are you who hunger now, for you shall be satisfied" (Luke 6:20, 21). *Shall be* satisfied. One day there will be no hunger and no famine. But that day is not yet.

2. Whenever one of God's creatures enjoys a morsel of food, that creature delights in a gift of God. The Lord is and always will be the Provider, the Sustainer, the One who "has satisfied the thirsty soul, and the hungry soul He has filled with what is good" (Psalm 107:9). The only reason all of us do not die of starvation is that God is good and provides us with the food we need. As Paul said to the philosophers in Athens, "He Himself gives to all life and breath and all things" (Acts 17:25). Every day God spends more than the U.S. national treasury just to feed the hungry beaks of the sparrows around the world. So we shouldn't be surprised when we read in the Word of God that He is interested in our needs as well.

WHY DOES BREAD SUSTAIN US?

Matthew 4:4 says that man does not live by bread alone, but by every word that proceeds out of the mouth of God. There is more to that verse than the truth that spiritual things are more important than material things. Matthew also means that bread itself would have no value to us unless its value had been supplied by the Creator.

Why is it that bread meets the needs of the human body? How is it that the plants which grow from the earth have the ability to supply us with strength? How can they help us to grow? It is only possible through the word that proceeds out of the mouth of God. God speaks, and seed is given the nutritional properties we need to grow and become strong.

Were God to withdraw His word, bread would be useless to us; we might as well eat gravel. God has given the herbs of the field the nutrients which serve as fuel for our bodies. It is for good reason that the Bible says Christ "upholds all things by the word of His power" (Hebrews 1:3) and that "in Him all things hold together" (Colossians 1:17). It is the word of God that sustains us.

Here is an idea to think about:

Back of the loaf is the snowy flour
And back of the flour, the mill
And back of the mill is the field of wheat,
The rain, and the Father's will.[1]

We may put the ingredients together and pop the loaf into the oven, but if God hadn't put the flavor and nutrients into the seed, we'd end up with a useless piece of crust. The next time you sit down to a meal, look around the table. Trace the food back to the grocery store. Where did the store get it? And where did the mill get it before it went to the store? And where did it come from before that? Everything we have goes back to the bread God provides. He is the giver of all good things.

> Today was a good time in prayer. The particular burdens of my heart were heavy as I prayed. My own physical situation can dominate my thoughts if I allow it. These tests and my next treatment are very critical to my ultimate situation. I am also struggling with the nutrition part of all of this and need to spend more time in study. Lord, I love You and thank You so much for Your patience with me. I am committed to being Your servant and walking in fellowship with You. I do not want just a ministry that is blessed. I want my life to be blessed! Thank You for caring enough about me to see that I learn these lessons before it is too late!

The petition, "Give us this day our daily bread," encourages us to depend upon Him. I'm glad we bow and pray before we eat. We need to do so with awe and gratitude in our hearts. God is our provider, whether we acknowledge the fact or not.

A cute story illustrates the principle. A little boy from a Christian home was invited to his friend's house for dinner. When it was time to eat, everyone in the host's home just dug right in, without pausing to give thanks. The little boy looked up and asked, "Don't you pray before you eat?" The amused host answered, "Well, no, we don't." To which the little boy replied, "Oh. Neither does my dog," and picked up his own fork.

Dogs don't give thanks (at least so far as we know) because they don't understand. But we do understand. Every good thing we have comes from the gracious hand of God. If we have bread, it's because He gave it to us. And He instructs us to ask Him to continue to supply us with bread. Why? So that we might continue to recognize that our very lives depend on His goodness and grace.

EXAMINING THE DISCIPLINE OF OUR LIVES

Basically, what are our needs? Something to put on, something to put in, something to put over. God says He'll take care of that for us if we trust Him. And He wants us to ask Him for these things every day.

MUST WE ASK EVERY DAY?

"But Dr. Jeremiah," someone may say, "do you really think we are to ask God every day for the basic necessities of life? After all, the verse you just quoted says that the Father knows we need all these things. Are we to constantly petition God for the things He says He'll take care of?"

To answer this question we should return to Matthew 6:11. Remember that Jesus told us to ask for our *daily* bread. Not our weekly bread or our monthly bread or our yearly bread. D. L. Moody once said, "A man can no more take in a supply of grace for the future than he can eat enough for the next six months, or take sufficient air into his lungs at one time to sustain life for a week. We must draw upon God's boundless store of grace from day to day as we need it." Has not God promised to sustain us by His grace? Is it not true that we would die without it? And yet is it not equally true that we must consciously appropriate that grace every moment of every day? The daily bread for which we are instructed to pray is a tangible part of God's grace. God wants us to ask for it, not that He loves to hear us beg, but because He knows we have short memories and often forget that He is the One who supplies our every need. Praying for our *daily* bread eliminates pride and materialism, because we remember God hasn't promised us anything except to meet our needs. We need only pray every day for every day's bread.

Remember how the Israelites wandered in the wilderness and their bread rained down from heaven every day? They had to go out and collect enough bread for that day and were forbidden to collect any for the next day. If they did so anyway, their bread would spoil. The only day they could collect enough bread for two days was the day before the Sabbath, because the law forbade them to work on the Sabbath. On Friday they could collect enough bread for two days, and miracle of miracles, over that time the bread wouldn't spoil. But if they tried collecting bread for two days on Monday, thinking they could eat it on Tuesday, they wound up with a treat no one would want to pop into their mouths. God was very clear that His provision was a daily thing; His people were to trust Him one day at a time.

Jesus taught us to pray, "God, *today* I want Your will to be done on earth as it is in heaven, and I ask you to meet my needs *today*." The prayer presupposes that we talk to our Father every day. Could it be that one of the reasons some of us are on the week-to-week plan is that we talk to Him only once a week? We show up in church on Sunday and try to get all our praying done at once: "See you next week, Lord. Try to take care of these next seven days for me."

I believe in long range planning, but I'm not sure I believe in long range praying. Jesus is very clear in this verse about the need to pray anew each day. In fact, only here and in Luke 6:5 is the word "daily" found in the New Testament. It is the Greek word *epios,* which means "day to day." Give us today our daily bread.

When we trust the Lord day by day, we don't have to worry. What if He doesn't come through tomorrow? That's not our problem. We can talk to Him about tomorrow, tomorrow. Recently I read a couplet about worry that was written many years ago: "Better never trouble trouble 'til trouble troubles you, for you only make your trouble double trouble when you do." We are to combat worry by praying the way Jesus taught us: "Lord, this is my need for today. I don't know about tomorrow, but today I need Your provision in this specific way. Give me what I need today."

> *Today I read the third chapter in __Too Busy Not To Pray.__ "God is Able" was the title of the chapter. Bill Hybels developed a very interesting theme about why Christians don't pray. Basically his idea was born out of his own experience. We don't pray because down deep in our hearts beneath our surface faith, we don't believe that God can do anything about our requests. The whole chapter was a reminder that God is able to answer our prayers.*

ONLY WHAT WE NEED

Jesus doesn't teach us to pray, "Give us this day our daily steak" or "Give us this day our daily lobster." He says, "Give us this day our daily bread." I recently read an article that featured "The New Lord's Prayer," a felt-needs version:

> Our audience which art on earth,
> hallowed (or at least greatly esteemed) be our name.
> Our destiny come, our will be done in heaven as it is on earth.

Give us today our daily indulgences,

and help us to love and forgive ourselves just as we love and forgive others.

Lead us not into difficulty, suffering, or unhappiness, but deliver
us from unmet needs.

For ours is the kingdom, the power, and the glory, at least here
and now, which is what counts anyway.[2]

Harsh? Perhaps, but isn't it uncomfortably close to the way many of
us pray? The Lord's Prayer doesn't say, "Lord, give me everything I want."
It doesn't say, "Lord, I want all these things, and You are responsible to
give them to me." It says, "Give us this day our *daily bread*." It reminds
me of what Paul said to Timothy in the New Testament: "Godliness actually is a means of great gain, when accompanied by contentment…if we
have food and covering, with these we shall be content" (1 Timothy
6:6, 8). If you have what you need, and you have God, you have everything! Jesus said we are simply to ask God that our needs be met.

God has said He will give us what we *need*. God has not promised to
make us all wealthy. He has not promised to make us all healthy. Listen
to what Jim Bakker, the former head of the PTL network and a man who
formerly championed the health and wealth gospel, wrote in his book, *I
Was Wrong*, after being released from prison for defrauding scores of
financial contributors to his PTL empire:

During my time [in prison] I observed something that it seemed
to me had gotten nearly every inmate into trouble…. The under-
lying reason why some of the bankers, Wall Street businessmen,
doctors, and others, are in prison is because of something they
did to get more money. I realized that of the 60% of inmates who
were in prison because of drug-related crimes, most of them are
there not because of an addiction to drugs; they are there

because of an addiction to the drug of money. It was their insatiable desire for more money that led them to selling drugs in the first place, not a desire to ruin someone else's life, or get them hooked....

About the time of my parole hearing, I completed my study of all the words of Jesus in the New Testament.... Even the prodigal son, one of my favorite stories told by Jesus, took on new meaning as I read it for the first time with the overview of Scripture in mind. I quickly noticed that the story began with the younger brother saying to the father, "Give me! Give me my part of the inheritance" (Luke 15:12). He didn't even say, "Please give me." He simply demanded. Before long, that young man landed in the pigpen. I began to see that the fastest route to the pigpen begins with "Give me"...and the fastest route to the "big pen," the federal penitentiary, often begins with the same phrase, "Give me!"

For years I had embraced and espoused a gospel that some skeptics had branded as "prosperity gospel." I didn't mind the label; On the contrary, I was proud of it. "You're absolutely right!" I'd say to critics and friends alike. "I preach it, and I live it! I believe in a God who wants to bless his people...."

I even got to the point where I was teaching people at PTL, "Don't pray, 'God, Your will be done,' when you're praying for health or wealth. You already know it is God's will for you to have those things!... Instead of praying, 'Thy will be done,' when you want a new car, just claim it. Pray specifically and tell God what kind you want. Be sure to specify the options and what color you want, too." I may not always have been so blatant about it, but I often preached the prosperity message.

The more I studied the Bible, however, I had to admit that the prosperity message did not line up with the tenor of Scripture. My heart was crushed to think that I had led so many people astray. I was appalled that I could have been so wrong, and I was deeply grateful that God had not struck me dead as a false prophet!...

Many today believe that the evidence of God's blessing on them is a new car, a house, a good job, etc. But that is far from the truth of God's Word. If that be the case, then gambling casino owners, drug kingpins and movie stars are blessed of God. Jesus did not teach riches were a sign of God's blessing. In fact, Jesus said, "It is hard for a rich man to enter the Kingdom of Heaven."

If we equate earthly possessions and earthly relationships with God's favor, what are we to tell the billions of those living in poverty, or what do you do if depression hits, or what do you say to those who lose a loved one? Many "in name only" Christians would curse God if they lost all of their material possessions.

Jesus said, "Narrow is the way that leads to life and few there be that find it." It's time the call from the pulpit be changed from "Who wants the life of pleasure and good things, new homes, cars, materials and possessions, etc.?" to, "Who will come forward and accept Jesus Christ and the fellowship of His suffering?" Jesus calls us to come and die, die to ourselves and the world, so He might give us true life.[3]

Bakker's words are a powerful reminder that we must not take our Lord's invitation to ask for our daily bread and use it as license to start hopping around to all the donut shops in the world and saying, "God, I claim that, I claim that, I claim that..." God blesses some of us wonderfully, but with that blessing comes great responsibility. When God gives us more and more, it is so we can use more and more for His kingdom. He blesses us so we can bless others. As John Piper has written,

A wealth-and-prosperity doctrine is afoot today, shaped by the half-truth that says, "We glorify God with our money by enjoying thankfully all the things he enables us to buy. Why should a son of the King live like a pauper?" And so on. The true half of this is that we should give thanks for every good thing God enables us to have. That does glorify him. The false half is the subtle implication that God can be glorified in this way by all kinds of luxurious purchases.

If this were true, Jesus would not have said, "Sell your possessions and give alms" (Luke 12:33). He would not have said, "Do not seek what you are to eat and what you are to drink" (Luke 12:29). John the Baptist would not have said, "He who has two coats, let him share with who has none" (Luke 3:11). The Son of Man would not have walked around with no place to lay his head (Luke 9:58). And Zacchaeus would not have given half his goods to the poor (Luke 19:8).

God is not glorified when we keep for ourselves (no matter how thankfully) what we ought to be using to alleviate the misery of unevangelized, uneducated, unmedicated, and unfed millions. The evidence that many professing Christians have been deceived by this doctrine is how little they give and how much they own. God *has* prospered them. And by an almost irresistible law of consumer culture (baptized by a doctrine of health, wealth, and prosperity) they have bought bigger (and more) houses, newer (and more) cars, fancier (and more) clothes, better (and more) meat, and all manner of trinkets and gadgets and containers and devices and equipment to make life more fun.

They will object: does not the Old Testament promise that God will prosper his people? Indeed! God increases our yield so that by giving we can prove our yield is not our god. God does not prosper a man's business so he can move from a Ford to a

Cadillac. God prospers a business so that thousands of unreached peoples can be reached with the gospel. He prospers a business so that twelve percent of the world's population can move a step back from the precipice of starvation.[4]

So is making a big salary a sin? No. As Piper says again, "the issue is not how much a person makes. Big industry and big salaries are a fact of our times, and they are not necessarily evil. The evil is in being deceived into thinking a $100,000 salary must be accompanied by a $100,000 lifestyle. God has made us to be conduits of his grace. The danger is in thinking the conduit should be lined with gold. It shouldn't. Copper will do."[5]

ENLARGING OUR DUTY TO PRAY

In line with this, Jesus didn't teach us to pray, "Give *me* this day *my* daily bread," but "Give *us* this day *our* daily bread." There is a corporate side to this prayer that indicates we shouldn't be concerned merely about our own needs. This prayer is not only an antidote for pride, materialism, and worry, it's also the answer to selfishness. We are to pray, "Lord, as you meet my needs, also meet their needs."

Years ago a poet wrote:

Bow thy head and pray
That while thy brother starves today
Thou mayest not eat thy bread in ease.
Pray that no health or wealth or peace
May lull thy soul while the world lies
Suffering, and claims thy sacrifice.

WHAT KEEPS OUR PRAYERS FROM BECOMING SELFISH?

How do we keep our prayer for provision from becoming selfish? Very simply: We don't start praying at verse 11. We don't jump right in with,

"God, let me tell You what my needs are." Jesus teaches us to pray in sequence: "Our Father who art in heaven, hallowed be Thy name. Thy kingdom come. Thy will be done on earth as it is in heaven." How can we pray verse 11 selfishly and tritely and materialistically when we've just finished praying, "Thy will be done on earth as it is in heaven"? We can't! When we pray according to Jesus, our petition is in proper context: "Lord, in the context of Your will being done on this earth as it is in heaven, please meet the needs You know I have today."

The Bible says that some of us don't get our prayers answered because we ask amiss, that we might consume the answer on our own evil desires (see James 4:3). We don't have what we want because we want it for ourselves, not for God's sake. When we pray for our children, we ought not to pray for their health and their spirituality only so that we can be proud we have good kids. Instead, we should pray that our kids can be useful, meaningful tools in God's greater kingdom work. When we pray for a house, we shouldn't seek merely an edifice where we can live in comfort, but an instrument God can use to express His love and will on earth. It was Augustine who prayed, "he loves You too little who loves anything together with You which he loves not for Your sake." When we pray for the welfare of others in the context of our love for God, we can pray with great confidence that God will hear us and answer our prayers.

Years ago Oswald Chambers pointed out our tendency to err on this front when he wrote, "Instead of praying to the Lord of the harvest to send out laborers, we pray, 'O Lord, keep my body right; see after this matter and that for me.' Our prayers are taken up with our concerns, our own needs, and only once in a while do we pray for what He tells us to."[6] That's a stinging indictment, but I fear Chambers was right. One way to avoid such a charge is to make sure we follow our Savior's model and pray for corporate needs and not merely for our own.

One woman discovered she had trouble remembering to pray for the needs of others, so she devised a neat little memory trick:

Holding up her left hand, the woman explained: "When I'm ready to pray, I look at my hand. This reminds me to pray for those near me—my family, my friends, my neighbors."

Pointing to her index finger, she added: "My teachers used to point at us in school. Sometimes the preacher points at us, so as I come to this finger, I pray for my teachers, the preachers, and others who have been my guides.

"My middle finger is my largest one. It stands above the others. This brings to mind the rulers of our country, the officials of our city. So I pray for them.

"The next finger is called the weak finger. When I come to it I think of the weak, the sick, those who are poor and need help. I ask God to help them."

Coming to her little finger, she concluded: "Last is my little finger. This stands for me. I finish praying for myself and the things I need."[7]

Such "five finger praying" is a clever way to apply our Lord's instruction to pray, "Give us this day our daily bread." When our bread gets spread around the community and the world, God is glorified. And He is very, very pleased.

BE UTTERLY ASTOUNDED!

I love the text from Habakkuk 1:5, which says, "Look among the nations and watch—be utterly astounded! For I will work a work in your days which you would not believe, though it were told you" (NKJV). God loves to do astounding things. And most of the time, He does those things in response to the prayers of His people.

George Mueller knew all about asking for bread and he saw God provide time after time in astonishing ways. I treasure the poem he crafted in response to God's faithfulness. I love it because it's true, and I love it because it encourages me to pray for my own daily bread as well as the bread of others in my circle. See if it resonates as much with you as it does with me:

> I believe God answers prayer,
> Answers always, everywhere
> I may cast my anxious care,
> Burdens I could never bear,
> On the God who heareth prayer.
> Never need my soul despair
> Since He bids me boldly dare
> To the secret place repair,
> There to prove He answers prayer.[8]

Chapter Eight

PERSONAL
RELATIONSHIPS:

LIVING IN THE JOY OF FORGIVENESS

"Forgive us our debts as we forgive our debtors."

Many years ago Simon Wiesenthal, a former prisoner in a
Nazi concentration camp and a crusader to bring the per-
petrators to judgment, wrote a book called *The Sunflower*.
At the beginning of his book Wiesenthal describes an experience he had
one afternoon in Poland. Author Lewis Smedes recounts it in his own
book, *Forgive & Forget*:

> He had been assigned to clean the rubbish out of a hospital that
> the Germans had improvised for wounded soldiers carried in from
> the Eastern Front. A nurse walked over to him, out of nowhere,
> took his arm, ordered him to come with her, and led him upstairs,
> along a row of stinking wounded, to the side of a bed where a
> young soldier, his head wrapped in yellow, pus-stained bandages,
> was dying. He was maybe twenty-two, an SS trooper.
>
> The soldier, whose name was Karl, reached out and grabbed
> Wiesenthal's hand, clamped it as if he feared Wiesenthal would

run away. He told Wiesenthal that he had to speak to a Jew. He had to confess the terrible things he had done so that he could be forgiven. Or he could not die in peace.

What had he done? He was fighting in a Russian village where a few hundred Jewish people had been rounded up. His group was ordered to plant full cans of gasoline in a certain house. Then they marched about two hundred people into the house, crammed them in until they could hardly move. Next they threw grenades through the windows to set the house on fire. The soldiers were ordered to shoot anyone who tried to jump out of a window.

The young soldier recalled, "Behind the window of the second floor, I saw a man with a small child in his arms. His clothing was alight. By his side stood a woman, doubtless the mother of the child. With his free hand, the man covered the child's eyes—then he jumped into the street. Seconds later, the mother followed. We shot...Oh, God...I shall never forget it— it haunts me."

The young man paused and then he said, "I know that what I have told you is terrible. I have longed to talk about it to a Jew and beg forgiveness from him. I know that what I am asking is almost too much, but without your answer I cannot die in peace."

Silence! The sun was high in heaven. God was somewhere. But here, two strangers were all by themselves, caught in the crisis of forgiveness. A member of the super race begged to be forgiven by a member of the condemned race.

Wiesenthal tells us what he did. "I stood up and looked in his direction, at his folded hands. At last, I made up my mind, and without a word I left the room." The German went to God unforgiven by man.

Wiesenthal survived the concentration camp. But he could

not forget the SS trooper. He wondered, troubled, for a long time, whether he should have forgiven the soldier. He told the story in his book, *The Sunflower*, and ended it with an awful question for every reader: "What would you have done?"[1]

The rest of Wiesenthal's book is a collection of essays by people who answer the question: Would they have forgiven the soldier? Some said yes, some said no. Suppose you were assigned to write one of those chapters. What would you have done if asked to extend such a costly forgiveness?

SOME FORGIVENESS SEEMS UNFAIR

Some people don't need a story like Wiesenthal's to tell them that the concept of forgiving seems unfair. Lewis Smedes recounts what happened to Jane Graafschap:

> Jane and her husband, Ralph, had finally brought their children through the crazy maze of adolescence, and gently pushed them out of the house. Jane was glad they had flown the coop; finally she was going to have a life of her own, get back on her own track and make something of herself.
>
> But a family tragedy stopped her. Ralph's younger brother and his wife were killed in a car crash, and left three children, ages eight, ten, and twelve, all by themselves. Ralph had a strong sense of duty; he knew it was his sacred calling to take his brother's orphaned children in. Jane was too compassionate or too tired to disagree, she never did know which. She took them in, not for a month, but for the duration. As for Ralph, he was gone a lot, a traveling man, on the road, making deals. Nine years groan by. Two of the kids are gone; The only one still home is seventeen, his mind bent slightly out of shape but functional. In a few years, Jane and Ralph would be home free.

Not quite. Jane's body had gotten a little lumpy by this time, while Ralph's secretary, Sue, was a dazzler; besides, Sue really understood his large male needs. How could he help falling in love? He and Sue knew that their love was too true to be denied and too powerful to be resisted. So, Ralph divorced Jane and he married Sue.

Ralph and Sue were very happy, and they dunked their happiness in a warm, religious froth; their convivial, accepting church celebrated their new-found joy with them. They were kept afloat in togetherness by their affirming Christian community. But Ralph needed one more stroke of acceptance. So he called Jane to ask her to forgive him, and be glad with him that he was finally a happy man. "I want you to bless me," he said.

"I want you to go to hell," she replied. What? Forgive? Throw away the only power she had—the strength of her hate, the energy of her contempt? Her contempt was her power, her dignity, her self-esteem. It was unfair to ask her to forgive. The least the louse deserved was the steady stream of her scorn.[2]

Smedes probably speaks for many of us when he says, "There is a lot to be said for *not* forgiving people... Why should people cut and thrust their way through our lives, leaving us bleeding in their wake, and then expect us to forgive everything and act as if nothing went wrong? Forgiving *is* an outrage against...dues-paying morality."[3]

Then we read our Lord's words: "Forgive us our debts as we forgive our debtors." And we wonder: *Was He serious?*

A MOST DIFFICULT TRICK

It is interesting that the Lord moved immediately in His prayer from "give us" to "forgive us." "Give us our daily bread," He says, "And forgive us our debts…" Instead of "debts," other translations use the word "trespasses" or "sins."

A case could be made that this is the most important phrase in the Lord's Prayer. It is the only phrase that He repeats for emphasis. At the end of the prayer, in verses 14–15, Jesus revisits this discussion. He says, "For if you forgive men for their transgressions, your heavenly Father will also forgive you. But if you do not forgive men, then your Father will not forgive your transgressions." This business of forgiveness is so important, Jesus adds a two-verse commentary on it.

> *Today I read from Oswald Chambers that we need to deal with relationships in the context of intercession. We often think that we need to meet with people in order to help them, but "miracles" are in the prayer closet, and we should never replace our worship time with working out problems with others in meetings.*

His words have theological ramifications that cause our minds to struggle. What does He mean? Is my forgiveness of my friend the condition upon which God forgives me? Or is my unwillingness to forgive an indication that God does not really live in my heart?

THE NATURE OF TRUE FORGIVENESS

In order to understand Matthew 6:12, 14 and 15, we have to turn to Matthew 18, where Jesus tells a story about the nature of true forgiveness:

> Then Peter came and said to Him, "Lord, how often shall my brother sin against me and I forgive him? Up to seven times?" Jesus said to him, "I do not say to you, up to seven times, but up to seventy times seven.
>
> "For this reason the kingdom of heaven may be compared to a certain king who wished to settle accounts with his slaves.

And when he had begun to settle them, there was brought to him one who owed him ten thousand talents. But since he did not have the means to repay, his lord commanded him to be sold, along with his wife and children and all that he had, and repayment to be made. The slave therefore falling down, prostrated himself before him, saying, 'Have patience with me, and I will repay you everything.' And the lord of that slave felt compassion and released him and forgave him the debt.

"But that slave went out and found one of his fellow slaves who owed him a hundred denarii; and he seized him and began to choke him, saying, 'Pay back what you owe.' So his fellow slave fell down and began to entreat him, saying, 'Have patience with me and I will repay you.' He was unwilling however, but went and threw him in prison until he should pay back what was owed.

"So when his fellow slaves saw what had happened, they were deeply grieved and came and reported to their lord all that had happened. Then summoning him, his lord said to him, 'You wicked slave, I forgave you all that debt because you entreated me. Should you not also have had mercy on your fellow slave, even as I had mercy on you? And his lord, moved with anger, handed him over to the torturers until he should repay all that was owed him.

"So shall My heavenly Father also do to you, if each of you does not forgive his brother from your heart." (Matthew 18:21–35)

The servant who owed ten thousand talents was in more debt than any of us (we hope) will ever be. One talent was worth about six thousand days' work, so it would have taken this man thirteen years, working six days a week, to earn *one* talent. And he owed ten thousand of them! How could a servant get in that kind of trouble? Was he pilfering from the treasury? Did he make a bad investment? We don't know and it doesn't matter to the story. What we do know is that he owed a gigantic amount and had nothing with which to pay it. It would have been understandable if his king had laughed in his face when he begged to be given time to repay his debt in full. He would have to live 130,000 years and put every dime he ever earned into his debt to pay it off. The man was a fool no matter how you look at it and the king easily could have reacted in anger. And yet he was moved with compassion and let the servant go, debt free.

The king not only was compassionate, but he understood the magnitude of the servant's problem. There was no way the king was going to get paid, so he simply forgave his servant.

Not much later this same servant found one of his peers who owed him a little money, about three months' work. Peanuts! Yet the one who had been forgiven many lifetimes' worth of debt grabbed this guy by the neck and demanded, "Pay me what you owe me!" When the indebted servant couldn't pay up immediately, the forgiven servant had him thrown in prison. As soon as the other servants heard what happened, they told the king, who called the evil man on the carpet, blasted him, and gave him the full punishment he deserved.

What was Jesus teaching us through this parable? The king represents God; the servant is all of us. We owe a debt of sin we could not possibly repay. Our little attempts to pay our debt would be like those of the servant offering to pay his huge debt. It's ridiculous! We have nothing in our account but zeroes! And yet, because of His great love, God forgave us our astronomical debt. Now the question is, will we be like the evil servant—someone who wants to take all the forgiveness God can give, but is not willing to give it to somebody else?

Lewis Smedes makes some stinging comments about the parable:

> Jesus grabs the hardest trick in the bag—forgiving—and says we
> have to perform it or we are out in the cold, way out, in the

boondocks of the unforgiven. He makes us feel like the miller's daughter who was told that if she didn't spin gold out of a pile of straw before morning, she would lose her head. And no Rumpelstiltskin is going to come in and spin forgiving out of our straw hearts. But why is Jesus so tough on us?

He is tough because the incongruity of sinners refusing to forgive sinners boggles God's mind. He cannot cope with it; there is no honest way to put up with it.

So he says: "if you want forgiving from God and you cannot forgive someone who needs a little forgiving from you, forget about the forgiveness that you want." [4]

Is that tough, or is that tough? Does Jesus mean that unforgiveness indicates an unregenerate heart? If we remain unwilling to forgive our friends and enemies, does that mean we have never truly come to faith in Christ? *It may.*

SOBERING, FRIGHTENING WORDS

If you consider yourself a Christian but are stubbornly refusing to forgive someone who has hurt you, perhaps you need to hear again Jesus' words at the close of His parable: "And his lord, moved with anger, handed him over to the torturers until he should repay all that was owed him." Remember, we have already identified this "lord" with God. And how does this lord react to the one who refused to forgive? He burned "with anger" against him. And how was this anger displayed? The king handed the unforgiving man over to the "torturers" in prison. For how long? For good. It is clear the man will never get out, for if he couldn't pay while he was outside the prison and able to work, how would he manage to pay while on the inside with no job? One last question: What place do you think the prison in Jesus' story represents?

Yet even with that, Jesus is not quite through with us. Ponder the

Lord's concluding words as He applies His own story: "So shall My heavenly Father also do to you, if each of you does not forgive his brother from your heart."

Sobering words! Frightening words! Words too sobering and frightening to be dismissed or softened. While I would never suggest that someone might lose his or her salvation by committing some sin—it is by grace, through faith, that we are saved, and our salvation depends wholly on the finished work of Christ on the cross and nothing else—yet I would be equally loathe to give confidence to an unsaved person that he or she was right with God. This parable appears to teach that if we willfully harbor unforgiveness in our hearts, the reason may be that the Holy Spirit does not live there. And according to Romans 8:9, "if anyone does not have the Spirit of Christ, he does not belong to Him." Jesus cannot conceive how a regenerate man or woman—a person whose sins caused Him to be nailed to a cross—could then turn around and refuse to forgive a debt infinitely smaller by comparison. If unforgiveness fills our heart, it seems clear the Holy Spirit does not.

And yet... Do you know any Christians who are unforgiving? If you hang out in the church as I do, you're bound to meet all kinds of Christians with grudges. I consider them real believers. What can we say of them? Let me suggest another side to forgiveness that we ought to consider.

FORGIVE IN ORDER TO BE FORGIVEN

One kind of forgiveness to which Jesus is calling us in Matthew 6 and 18 is what I call "relational forgiveness." An illustration might help to explain what I mean.

When I was a teenager, I was fascinated with the idea of driving long before I was legally allowed to drive. One day my father left his Chrysler sitting in the driveway. He tempted me—he put the keys on the table. Nobody was home. I decided this was my opportunity to take that car out for a spin.

I didn't want to motor down a highly traveled street, so I found a gravel road out in the country. I was tooling along when I saw a farmer in his truck approaching me. He decided to take his half of the lane out of the middle and flat ran me off the road! Now I had my dad's new Chrysler in the ditch, and I freaked out. I thought about running away from home. I thought about suicide.

Finally a guy pulled me out with his tractor. Somehow I got that car home, complete with one side all smashed up. If I remember correctly, I had to keep turning left; I couldn't turn right. Somehow I got the thing in the driveway and waited for the inevitable. I died a thousand deaths in those hours while I waited for my dad to come home.

I was watching through the window when he arrived. He stood and stared at the car, shook his head, walked in and asked, "David, did you do that?"

"Yeah, I did."

He shook his head again. My dad normally responded in a more forceful way. This time he just kept shaking his head and walked into the other room. He didn't talk. Not at supper, not at breakfast, not at lunch, not at supper the next night. O, it was awful!

Finally it hit me: This was my fault. I had to fix this. So, I went to see him at work and said, "Dad, I've got to tell you I feel terrible about what I did. I was wrong, deceitful, dishonest. I knew better than to do that. I'm sorry, and I want to ask you to forgive me."

"You're forgiven," he said. "And you will pay for the car."

Now, when I wrecked my dad's car, did I cease to be my father's son? No. But our working relationship was in deep trouble. In order to be restored, I had to ask forgiveness for my actions and my dad had to extend it. I had to repent, and true repentance required paying for the car.

If we want to know oneness with the Lord in our daily relationship with Him, if we want to feel a closeness when we pray to God, we can't hold grudges against others. If we did, how could we come to God and say, "Father, I just love being forgiven, and it's wonderful to talk to you"? The Bible clearly says that if we come to the altar and remember that someone has something against us, or if we have something against someone else, we must go find our brother, be reconciled to him, and only *then* come back and talk to God. I like the way Eugene Peterson has rendered this in *The Message*:

> This is how I want you to conduct yourself in these matters. If you enter your place of worship and, about to make an offering, you remember a grudge a friend has against you, abandon your offering, leave immediately, go to this friend and make things right. Then and only then, come back and work things out with God.
>
> Or say you're out on the street and an old enemy accosts you. Don't lose a minute. Make the first move, make things right with him. After all, if you leave the first move to him, knowing his track record, you're likely to end up in court, maybe even jail. If that happens, you won't get out without a stiff fine. (Matthew 5:21–26; see also Mark 11:25)

If we want to enjoy relational harmony with God, we must forgive those who have wronged us. Lord Herbert put it very well when he wrote, "He who cannot forgive others breaks the bridge over which he himself must someday pass."[5]

"But they hurt me!" you cry.

I will not deny it. But the only way to heal the pain that will not heal itself is to forgive the person who hurt you. Forgiving heals your memory as you change your memory's vision. When you release the wrongdoer from your wrath, you cut a malignant tumor out of your own life. You set a prisoner free...and you discover that the prisoner you freed was yourself.

American theologian Reinhold Niebuhr saw this after World War II when he said, "We must finally be reconciled to our foe lest we perish in the vicious circle of hatred." And I think it was comedian Buddy Hackett who said, "I've had a few arguments with people, but I never carry a grudge. You know why? While you're carrying a grudge, they're out dancing."

FOUR STEPS TO FORGIVING OTHERS

How do you forgive? Do you do it flippantly? Do you extend it because it's "the right thing to do," even though you don't mean it? Or do you forgive when you're still dying inside but pretend you're not hurt? Biblical forgiveness never overlooks the injury. Lewis Smedes says it well:

> The act of forgiving, by itself, is a wonderfully simple act; but it always happens in a storm of complex emotions. It is the hardest trick in the whole bag of personal relationships.
>
> So let us be honest with each other. Let us talk plainly about the "magic eyes" that are given to those who are ready to be set free from the prison of pain they never deserved.
>
> We forgive in four stages. If we can travel through all four stages, we achieve the climax of reconciliation.
>
> The first stage is *hurt*: when somebody causes you pain so deep and so unfair that you cannot forget it, you are pushed into the first stage of the crisis of forgiving.[6]

None of us has escaped the hurt from sins committed against us. Someone might think, *If you're a Christian, you take all these things in stride.* No! You still hurt. Don't be afraid of it; that is part of the process. I am so tired of Christian teachers and preachers taking the truth of the Bible and using it to erase the truth of life. The truth of life is what the Bible is all about, and the Bible does not say that when we are hurt we are not supposed to feel it.

Step number two, according to Smedes, is *hate*. "That can't be godly," you say. I didn't say it was godly; I said it was step number two. In this stage you can't shake the memory of how much you were hurt. You can't wish your enemy well. Sometimes you want the person who hurt you to suffer like you suffered. You want him to hurt and you think of ways to do it; you construct speeches in your mind; you come up with plans to run over him when you see him on the highway.

The third stage is *healing*. You are given the "magic eyes" to see the person who hurt you in a new light. Your memory heals. You turn back the flow of pain and you are free again.

The fourth stage is the *coming together*. You invite the person who hurt you back into your life. If he or she repents and comes honestly, love can move you toward a new and healed relationship. The fourth stage depends on the person you forgive as much as it depends on you. Sometimes he doesn't come back and you have to heal all alone. But you can get healed.

In his book *The Tender Touch of God*, Mike MacIntosh tells about a visit to Singapore in which he was allowed to speak with death row inmates awaiting execution. One man was a nineteen year old scheduled to hang in two weeks for murder. In prison the young man had come to faith in Christ, but he told Mike, "I know that I am saved from my sin. I know that when I am hung and my neck breaks that I will go to heaven. But still I am mad." When Mike asked why, the man told him that he had killed only one man in a drug deal; his friends had murdered two others, but he had been convicted of all three killings. He thought that was unfair. "I told him to forgive his buddies and to spend the next two weeks forgiving...those who had hurt him. I also suggested he spend the next two weeks reading the Bible and praying," Mike wrote.[7]

Some time later Mike found out that discrepancies had been found in the court transcripts and the young man was brought before a judge once more. The man told the judge that he was guilty of one murder, not three, but that he had forgiven his friends and was no longer bitter at the court. He told the judge that Jesus Christ had come into his heart, forgiven him his sins and given him great peace of heart; whatever the judge decided was in God's hands. The judge took another look at the transcripts, ruled a mistrial, and released the young man. "The last I was told," Mike wrote, "the young man was so elated and grateful to God that he became an evangelist, went across the border into Malaysia, and is preaching the gospel to the Muslims."8

> *Lord, I read something out of my journal yesterday that reminded me that many of the relationships that I have—and there are so many, as is proven by the number of names in the index of the journal—Lord, many of these relationships have got to be dealt with through intercession and not personal involvement. I cannot carry on these relationships through the expense of time and energy, for there is not enough to go around. But, Lord, please help me to pray for these people, and to have a plan that would allow me to do so.*

Jesus says that those who live by God's forgiveness must imitate it. A person whose only hope is that God will not hold his faults against him forfeits his right to hold others' faults against them. "Do as you would be done by" is the rule here. The unforgiving "Christian" brands himself as a hypocrite (or worse). Jesus Himself stresses that only those who grant forgiveness will receive it.

"Can I do this?" you ask. *Not in your own strength.* Forgiveness is not natural, it is supernatural. But if the Holy Spirit indwells you, you have all the resources you need. You must simply choose to appropriate them.

FORGIVE BEFORE YOU NEED TO BE FORGIVEN

I dare you to pray like this every morning: "God, I don't know the things that will happen to me today. Maybe some of them will be bad. Sometime today someone will probably hurt me, but I forgive them already. One thing I'm sure of: Nothing will happen to me today that will require a forgiveness like the kind You have already granted me. Thank You for Your forgiveness. Help me to forgive as I have been forgiven."

In your prayer each day you can build the foundation of a forgiving spirit even before you have been injured. You can ask God to help you each day to see the incredible debt He has paid on your behalf. You can ask Him to help you imitate the sacrificial love that cost Him so dearly.

It is not often that a poet can capture the essence of Scripture, but I think this one did:

Forgive our sins as we forgive
        You taught us, Lord, to pray.
But You alone can grant us grace
        To live the words we say.
How can Your pardon reach and bless
        The unforgiving heart
That broods on wrongs and will not let
        Old bitterness depart?
In blazing light, Your cross reveals
        The truth we dimly knew:
How small the debts men owe to us;
        How great our debt to You.
Lord, cleanse the depths within our souls.
        And bid resentment cease.
Then reconciled to God and man,
        Our lives will spread Your peace.[9]

That's it, isn't it? God loves to forgive us, and He loves it when we forgive others. Perhaps you have some homework to do—maybe in person, maybe on the phone or in writing. If you remember what God has done for you, you will find the power to extend that same forgiving love to those who have hurt you.

FORGIVE JUST AS YOU ARE FORGIVEN

When we understand how much God has forgiven us, we are set free to forgive others. That's Jesus' whole point in this part of the Lord's Prayer and in His two-verse commentary afterward. We are constantly to reflect upon the fact that we have been forgiven much. Remember the sinful woman in Luke 7 who crashed a party at Simon the Pharisee's house in order to anoint Jesus' feet with tears and perfume and wipe them with her hair? Jesus forgave her and said, "For this reason I say to you, her sins, which are many, have been forgiven, for she loved much; but he who is forgiven little, loves little" (Luke 7:47). Simon did not see himself as a great sinner, but the truth (of course) was that his sins were as great as the woman's. Because he did not have a sordid past, Simon did not think he needed much forgiveness. He was wrong.

It is so easy to fall into the trap which ensnared Simon. Some of us were saved while growing up in Christian homes, and if we didn't live a sordid life, we may not realize how much we have been forgiven. One cure for that is to read the first four chapters of Romans a couple of times. Paul makes it clear God has forgiven us a tremendous debt we could never pay.

When we accept Jesus Christ, His blood that was shed on the cross is applied to our account, and we are justified. Our sins are placed on Jesus and His righteousness is placed on us, so that when God looks at us, He sees us as righteous and holy. Our justification is a point-in-time-forgiveness, a judicial act that God decrees when we ask Christ into our heart. He credits us with the righteousness of Jesus. We don't have any right to it, but through faith and because of grace, God says, "I declare you righteous." We are judicially forgiven.

And how did God forgive us? For Christ's sake, He forgave us unconditionally. He forgave us freely. He didn't say, "I'll forgive you—but I won't forget how bad you are!" When He forgave our sin, He threw it into the deepest part of the sea and put up a sign saying, "No fishing here!" He put our sin behind His back, as far as the east is from the west. He annulled it. He took it out. He nailed it to the cross.

> *Lord, help me today to once again spend my quality hours looking to You and pursuing a relationship with You. As Charles Stanley said this morning, if we go through our whole lives and do not learn to pursue a relationship with You, then we have lost the real purpose of our living, and we will end our lives in disappointment and a sense of failure. Lord, if what he said is true, then surely there are so many of us, and many more so than me, that are wasting their lives as Christians. I want to find meaning and purpose in the things that You have called me to do, and I know that this process starts in "pursuing a relationship with God." Lord, help me today to be a pursuer!*

Now, while we cannot remove the guilt of anyone's sin—God alone does that—we are called upon to forgive freely those who have wronged us, just as God freely forgave us. We must not require that someone jump through fifteen hoops and seven public penances before we condescend to forgive them. We are to extend forgiveness to others in the same way that God did to us: Unconditionally.

THE ULTIMATE TRIUMPH OVER EVIL

Forgiveness prompted by love is the only way to repair the devastation that so often mars our relationships. Healing can come in no other way—to us or to the people who have hurt us. As Philip Yancey wrote in his bestseller *The Jesus I Never Knew:*

> Here are the words of M.: "I cannot be any more specific about the methodology of love than to quote these words of an old

priest who spent many years in battle. 'There are dozens of ways to deal with evil and several ways to conquer it. All of them are facets of the truth that the only ultimate way to conquer evil is to let it be smothered within a willing, living human being. When it is absorbed there like blood in a sponge or a spear into one's heart, it loses its power and goes no further.' The healing of evil—scientifically or otherwise—can by accomplished only by the love of individuals. A willing sacrifice is required.... I do not know how this occurs. But I know that it does.... Whenever this happens there is a slight shift in the balance of power in the world."[10]

Are you willing to allow that "slight shift in the balance of power in the world" to begin with you? In His prayer, Jesus calls us not only to reach out to God for His forgiveness, but also to reach out to others and extend to them our own. That is the only ultimate way to conquer evil. Our willing sacrifice is required. Evil will be healed only through the love of individuals—that is, through you and me.

And it can start today.

Chapter Nine

PROTECTION:

SEEKING SAFETY FROM HARM

"Do not lead us into temptation, but deliver us from evil."

E ver heard the story about the minister who parked his car in a no-parking zone in a large city? He was short on time and couldn't find an open space with a meter, so he put a note under his windshield wiper that said, "I have circled the block ten times. If I don't park here, I'll miss my appointment. 'Forgive us our trespasses.'"

When he returned he found a citation from a police officer along with this note: "I've circled this block for ten years. If I don't give you a ticket, I'll lose my job. 'Lead us not into temptation.'"

A PERPLEXING PETITION

This section of the Lord's Prayer has probably caused more head-scratching than any other. Certainly it has prompted commentators to suggest more possible interpretations than any other part of this prayer. The words almost immediately perplex us: "Do not lead us into temptation." What could those enigmatic words of Jesus mean?

We all understand that it is God's nature to feed us and to forgive us. But is it God's nature to lead us into temptation? Why do we have to ask God to refrain from doing something we're pretty sure He would never do in the first place? Can a holy, righteous, pure, undefiled, blameless, unblemished, virtuous God ever lead *anyone* into temptation? That's a question which has been asked for a long time:

> Historical records show that from as early as the second century Christians were already asking this obvious question. The African theologian Tertullian, commenting on the Lord's Prayer in about A.D. 192, bristled at the notion that God could tempt us. "Far be the thought," he wrote, "that the Lord should seem to tempt, as if He were either ignorant of [the limits] of someone's faith, or else eager to overthrow [that faith]."[1]

To add to the confusion, consider James 1:12–15 (NKJV):

> Blessed is the man who endures temptation; for when he has been approved, he will receive the crown of life which the Lord has promised to those who love him. Let no one say when he is tempted, 'I am tempted by God'; for God cannot be tempted by evil, nor does He Himself tempt anyone. But each one is tempted when he is drawn away by his own desires and enticed. Then, when desire has conceived, it gives birth to sin; and sin, when it is full grown, brings forth death.

At first glance, what Jesus taught in the Lord's Prayer and what James taught in his epistle seem to contradict one another. On one hand, we read in James that God never tempts anybody to sin. But on the other hand, in Matthew Jesus tells us that every day when we pray, we are to ask God not to lead us into temptation. How do we put these two statements together?

THE CONNECTION BETWEEN TRIALS AND TEMPTATIONS

First, we should note that the word for "temptation" in the New Testament is the Greek term *peirasmus*. The term basically means "a test" or "a trial." When we use the word "temptation" in English we almost always understand it to mean a seduction to evil; but the Greek word is neutral. In James 1:2 and 12, this word is used one way: "My brethren, count it all joy when you fall into various trials…." and "Blessed is the man who endures temptation" (NKJV). The words translated "trials" and "temptation" come from the same term in Greek, *peirasmus*, and in these verses it refers to the common trials we face in life. In verse 13, however, the same word is used in a totally different way: "Let no one say when he is tempted, 'I am tempted by God'…." This time the word "temptation," *peirasmus*, refers to an enticement to evil. Context alone determines the meaning of the term.

By the way, this isn't as odd as it may appear. We do the same thing in English all the time. Consider the word "bag," for instance. "Bag" can have several distinct meanings, depending upon context. If I were to say, "I *bagged* the squirrel right over there, pal. I put him in that *bag* on the picnic table. I sure hope Martha isn't upset with me—the old *bag*. I can see the puffy red *bags* under her eyes already. But I suppose it's too late to hide—the cat's already out of the *bag*," could you follow my train of thought? In that one paragraph alone the word "bag" is used five times, each time in a different sense. You understood my meaning in each case by the context in which the word appeared. It's the same situation in Greek.

These two things—trials and enticements—are closely related. Often it is in the midst of a *trial* that you face a *temptation* to do the wrong thing. When you're under financial pressure and you don't know if you have enough money to pay your taxes, that pressure can translate into a temptation, an enticement, a desire to do evil by cheating the IRS. We shouldn't be surprised that the same word can be used to describe both a trial and a temptation.

TWO POSSIBLE OUTCOMES

Whenever we go through a trial or a test, we will either pass or fail. Tests in school can result in either a passing or a failing grade. When God brings a trial into our lives, there is always the possibility that the trial can be turned into a temptation to do evil. For instance, many years after Joseph was kidnapped by his brothers and sold into slavery in Egypt, he and his brothers met again after Joseph had become Prime Minister of the Egyptian empire. It would have been a perfect opportunity for Joseph to punish his brothers for their mistreatment of him; in that sense, it was a trial. Would Joseph do wrong in return for the wrong done him? Joseph declared to his brothers, "You meant evil against me, but God meant it for good" (Genesis 50:20). In that story are pictured the two concepts we have been reviewing.

But back to Matthew. We can safely assume when we read Jesus' words that the one thing He is *not* saying is that God would ever entice us to sin. God would never set us up to fall into a sink hole. It simply is not God's nature to do that; He is incapable of it. James says God is not tempted by evil and that He cannot tempt anyone with evil.

So what does Jesus mean when He tells us to pray, "Lord, don't lead us *into* temptation"? If God will not Himself entice us to sin, would He lead us into a place where we could be enticed? Does that ever happen? Did it ever happen? Is that different from tempting us outright?

Absolutely, on all counts.

Remember how Jesus was tempted: "Then Jesus was led up by the Spirit into the wilderness to be tempted by the devil" (Matthew 4:1). The Bible doesn't say He was led by the *devil* into the wilderness; it says He was led by the *Spirit of God* into the wilderness, and there He was tempted.

So does God ever allow *us* to be in a place where temptation can overtake us? Yes, He does. If you doubt it, consider Job. In his time Job was the most righteous man on the face of the earth, and one day Satan came to God and said, "Look at Job. He seems so righteous down there. But you let me have him for a while and I'll show You just how righteous he is!" So God gave Satan a long chain and told him, "OK, you can do this, but I will not permit you to kill him." Satan did everything he could but murder Job. He took his family, his flocks, everything he had on the earth. And don't forget, God gave His permission for all this. Wouldn't you rather that God would say, "From the moment you are saved, no more temptation for you"? Wouldn't that be great?

It would be, but that's not the way it is.

THE BENEFITS OF TEMPTATION

I think there are several reasons why temptation, even though we view it as negative, can have positive results when we submit ourselves to God.[2]

1. Temptation can reveal what is in our hearts

When Abraham went up the mountain to sacrifice his son Isaac, he was willing to do what God had told him to do. Still, it was a real test. He could have sinned. My temptation would have been to say, "I love this boy so much, I don't care what God said. I'm not taking his life!" But Abraham obeyed God and was ready to take Isaac's life, even though he didn't understand why God would ask such a horrible thing. On the way down the mountain, after God had spared Abraham the terrible loss, God said to him, in effect, "You always said you loved Me, but now I *know* you love Me." The same thing was true for Abraham. After this incident, he knew beyond a shadow of a doubt that he really loved God, because the trial revealed to him what was in his heart.

Temptation is frightening because it shows us how close we may be to sin. Temptation reveals to us who we are apart from God. Sometimes we need a startling reminder.

I know of a man who in his pre-Christian days was extremely promiscuous. By his second or third year of college he had already lost track of the number of women he had bedded. Shortly after he graduated he came to Christ, turned his back on his sexual immorality, and became a committed disciple. More than a dozen years passed. One day he was driving home on the freeway and noticed a car following him over several miles and through a number of lane changes. When he took an exit to get gasoline, the car followed. At the pump he watched as a young woman emerged from her fiery-red sports car. She approached him and said, "I saw you on the freeway and you looked like somebody who would be nice. I'm new to the area and would like to get to know you." She made it clear just how well she'd like to get to know him. Suddenly, all the old urges and patterns the man had known many years before started to reassert themselves. His wife wasn't there; who would know?

But just as suddenly the man was repulsed by the thoughts racing through his mind. How could he think such a thing, after following Christ for so many years? "No thanks—I'm married," he replied as he pointed to his ring. The girl drove off and the man was left shaking his head. He thought he was beyond such temptation; it was startling to realize he wasn't. He said a quick thank-you to God and drove home a much wiser man.

2. Temptation can refocus our deepest values

When Jesus was being tempted in the desert, Satan tried to get our Lord to use His power for His own benefit and to bow down and worship the devil in exchange for earthly power and splendor. He tried to get Jesus to avoid the cross and go right to the kingdom. What happened through that temptation? The Lord Jesus took a big, red marker and underscored the values in His life. He said, "No, no, no! By My response to this temptation you are going to see the values to which I'm committed."

We can meet temptation in the same way. For instance, those of us who travel for business are sometimes faced with temptations to act in ways we wouldn't in our "real" lives at home. What is God's purpose in allowing us to be tempted like this? Just like Jesus, we are given the opportunity to reexamine our deepest values. It is to be hoped that the value of our spouse, our children, our testimony, and our intimate relationship with our Father come right to the top. In the midst of temptation all of those things are underscored anew.

3. Temptation can reinforce our will

Through temptation, God sometimes grows us up. The Apostle Paul told Timothy, "Train yourself to be godly" (1 Timothy 4:7, NIV). Just as our physical muscles grow stronger through exercise, the muscle of our will is strengthened when we do the right thing. Every time we say no to temptation, the muscle of our will gets stronger and better able to say no the next time. On the other hand, every time we yield, the muscle is weakened. After we have walked with the Lord for a while, some things shouldn't tempt us like they once did. By building reserves of strength through resisting temptation, our will becomes more aligned with God's will.

4. Temptation can remind others of God's grace and goodness

What is the one character trait of Job that even our culture talks about? The *patience* of Job. How did he get that reputation? He got it through enduring severe trials. Some of us feel like we're living his book, that maybe the story of Job is being replayed in this world and we are the star players. Yet by reading Job's story of trials, temptation, and endurance, we find great encouragement for our own hearts. God continues today to use the story of a long-gone suffering servant to remind people of His grace and goodness in the midst of the most challenging ordeals.

Of course, if you read the book, it's clear that through most of his trials Job didn't think of God as either gracious or kind—yet by the end of the story, he realizes God was in control the whole time and that his feeble attempts to understand only sent him meandering down dead-ends. In the end, he realizes that his own painful cry of "Though He slay me, yet will I trust in Him" was really the wisest statement made by any human in the whole ordeal—and he finally experiences the grace and goodness of God when at last his fortunes are doubled.

A POSSIBLE CONTRADICTION

We have seen how temptation can actually be a positive thing in the lives of God's people. So why, then, would Jesus tell His disciples to pray that God would not lead them into it? Does this make any sense?

Yes, it does. It is possible to recognize the benefits of a difficult thing while still praying that it doesn't happen. In his commentary on Matthew, D.A. Carson points out at least two examples of this in the New Testament. First, while the Bible warns us that this age will be characterized by wars and rumors of wars (Matthew 24:6), yet it urges us to pray for those in authority so that "we may live peaceful and quiet lives" (1 Timothy 2:2, NIV). A contradiction? No. And even more compellingly, although Jesus Himself told His disciples to rejoice when persecuted (Matthew 5:10–12), He nevertheless instructed them to flee from it (Matthew 10:23) and even to pray that their journey would not be too severe (Matthew 24:20). So, as Carson says, "a prayer requesting to be spared testings may not be incongruous when placed beside exhortations to consider such testings, when they come, as pure joy."[3]

Without tests in school we wouldn't have learned as much. But does that mean we got up every morning and said, "O God, please bring on the tests today! Lord, may there be an exam in history today so I can grow and learn." Of course we prayed no such thing. What we did pray was, "Not today, Lord. O God, please not today!"

Why didn't we pray for tests in school? Because whenever we are given a test, there are only two possibilities: We can pass or we can fail. Tests can be good, but no one wants to take them all the time. Constant tests make us weary and more liable to fail. That's why Jesus encourages us to pray, "Lord, don't bring tests into our lives. Too many of them, and we risk failing and dishonoring You." Jesus told us to pray against temptations because, though tests can be useful, we are only limited human beings. We might fail the test. Divine deliverance is usually a better option!

In a sense, this petition is a beautiful confession of our own weakness, a realization of the truth, "Let him who thinks he stands take heed lest he fall" (1 Corinthians 10:12). And just consider the opposite of this prayer! Who would dare pray, "Lord, lead us into temptation"? I surely wouldn't. We all know deep in our hearts that when we face temptation, the possibility exists that we might not handle it well.

> *Lord, I have sensed the nearness of the Evil One in very recent days! I know that it is only Your hand of protection that keeps him from me. I would ask today that You would not allow me to be led into a tempting situation. I know that I am weak and that I could fall. I pray that You will deliver me from evil and from the Evil One. We are all candidates for discouragement if we are not careful.*

Yet when trials do come (as they will) and lead to temptation, we should use the occasion as an opportunity for growth. James says we should "count it all joy." Still, that doesn't mean we should pray for boatloads of the things. "Do not lead us into temptation" is a great prayer that recognizes our own weakness—and it also points us to our only reliable source of strength.

GOD IS IN THE DELIVERANCE BUSINESS

Fortunately for us, God is in the deliverance business. It was God who delivered Israel out of Egypt. It was God who delivered Daniel from the lions' den. It was God who delivered Esther from the evil Haman. It was

God who delivered David from the giant Goliath and Lot and his family from the city of Sodom. It was God who delivered Rahab from destruction and Deborah from the Philistines. It was God who delivered Elijah from Jezebel and Ahab. It was God who delivered the daughter of the Syro-Phoenician woman from demonic forces. It was God who delivered Peter from drowning and from prison. And it was God who delivered Paul from perils of every imaginable kind.

God is a deliverer. He loves for His children to pray for deliverance. He instructs us in Psalm 50:15, "Call upon Me in the day of trouble; I shall rescue you, and you will honor Me." A little later He says, "Because he has loved Me, therefore I will deliver him; I will set him securely on high, because he has known My name. He will call upon Me, and I will answer him; I will be with him in trouble; I will rescue him, and honor him" (Psalm 91:14–15). In fact, the only one I'm aware of that God refused to deliver was His own Son. He didn't deliver Jesus, but "delivered [Him] up because of our transgressions" so that we might be justified (Romans 4:25).

All this suggests an important question. Does this mean that when we pray for deliverance, we will always escape with our lives? Does it mean that praying for deliverance always guarantees us a happy ending?

Well, yes and no.

The answer is "yes" if by "escaping with our lives" we mean that eternal life is ours, right now, as a present gift. This is what Jesus meant in John 11:26 when He said to Martha after her brother Lazarus had died, "everyone who lives and believes in Me shall never die." How could He say such a thing with Lazarus cold and stinking in the tomb? Because in a much deeper sense, Lazarus was still alive. God *is* the God of Abraham, Isaac, and Jacob, and Jesus insisted that means He is the God of the living, not the dead. Everyone is alive to Him (including Lazarus in the grave). That is also why we can say that God always delivers us into happy endings; no other ending is possible in heaven. The great saints of Hebrews 11:37 who were "stoned," "sawn in two," and "put to death with the sword" were not delivered to a happy ending on this side of heaven—but of course, for the believer, that's not the end. That's just an entrance into pleasures at the right hand of God forevermore.

The answer is "no," however, if by "escaping with our lives" and a guaranteed "happy ending" we mean that we will always be spared hardship and death in this life. Remember, it was Jesus Himself who said that in this world we would have tribulation (John 16:33). It was the Master Himself who said His followers would be killed and crucified and flogged and persecuted from city to city (Matthew 23:34).

And yet it was also Jesus who instructed us to pray for deliverance. Was He talking about our ultimate deliverance to heaven? I don't think so. That deliverance was guaranteed the moment He arose from the grave. I believe He wants us to pray for deliverance from awful troubles in the here and now—even though occasionally He may decide in His sovereignty to let those troubles touch us. God *does* deliver His children in their present circumstances and He instructs us to pray for such deliverance, even though He may sometimes allow earthly troubles into our lives. I believe our attitude must be the same as that demonstrated by the three Hebrews just before they were thrown into the intense flames of Nebuchadnezzar's furnace: "If it be so, our God whom we serve is able to deliver us from the furnace of blazing fire; and He will deliver us out of your hand, O king. *But even if He does not*, let it be known to you, O king, that we are not going to serve your gods or worship the golden image that you have set up" (Daniel 3:17–18, emphasis added).

These godly men knew that God was able to deliver them from any deadly peril and they fully expected Him to do so. But they also recognized that God was sovereign and that He might have other plans for them; whatever the case, they would joyfully place their lives in His hands. That must also be our confidence. God is able to deliver us and we should expect Him to do so. We are instructed in the Lord's Prayer to ask that He deliver us. Yet He is sovereign and we must joyfully place our very lives in His hands. We can confidently pray for and expect to be delivered, even while we leave the final outcome to Him. This is not lack of faith; it is supreme trust in the One who is supremely trustworthy.

PRAYING FOR DAILY DELIVERANCE

When Jesus instructs us to pray daily for deliverance from evil, He is reminding us that danger is constant and always around us. The Anglicans of old certainly recognized this. In one of their prayer books this plea is found:

> From sin, from the crafts and assaults of the devil...from all blindness of heart; from pride, vain-glory and hypocrisy; from envy, hatred, and malice, and all uncharitableness...from fornication, and all other deadly sin; and from all the deceits of the world, and the flesh, and the devil...from sudden [unexpected and unprepared-for] death...from hardness of heart, and contempt of thy Word and Commandment, Good Lord, deliver us.[4]

The Psalmist was just as aware of his need for God's deliverance. David was a godly man with a heart for God. And yet the Psalms show us that David prayed often that God would deliver him. If we look into the kinds of things from which David prayed to be delivered, we can model our prayers for deliverance after his.

The six steps of temptation:

1. Deceit   3. Desire   5. Defeat
2. Delight   4. Deliberation   6. Despair

How can I overcome temptation?

1. Fight (James 4:7)
2. Follow (James 4:8)
3. Flee (2 Timothy 2:22; Romans 13:14)
4. Feed (Psalm 119:11)

1. Deliverance from persecution

> O LORD my God, in Thee I have taken refuge; Save me from all
> those who pursue me, and deliver me, lest he tear my soul like
> a lion, dragging me away, while there is none to deliver. (Psalm
> 7:1–2)

There were those who were out to get David for his faith. Paul
warned us, "indeed, all who desire to live godly in Christ Jesus will be
persecuted" (2 Timothy 3:12). Some of us who are serving God in secular environments are targets of persecution: Undermining, threats,
ridicule, scorn. David gives us permission to pray that we might be delivered from people who persecute us like this. And Paul took his advice:
"Pray...that we may be delivered from perverse and evil men," he asked
his friends in 2 Thessalonians 3:1, 2.

Jesus tells us in His Sermon on the Mount that we are blessed when
we are persecuted. But that does not mean that we should avoid praying to be delivered from the persecution. (Again, compare Matthew
5:10–12; 10:23; 24:20.) Jesus tells us to pray, "God, I don't know what's
going to happen today. I have no idea what they might say or how they
might attack me, but deliver me from my persecutors; deliver me from
evil."

2. Deliverance from peril and danger

> But you, O LORD, be not far off; O my Strength, come quickly
> to help me. Deliver my life from the sword, my precious life from
> the power of the dogs. Rescue me from the mouth of the lions;
> save me from the horns of the wild oxen. (Psalm 22:19–21, NIV)

In the vernacular of the Old Testament, acts of the sword, dogs, lions
and wild oxen are the kinds of random, senseless tragedies that could

happen to anyone. Today, we too deal with all kinds of random, sense-less violence. We can pray like David, "Lord, deliver me from the awful things that happen to people in this evil world. Deliver me from peril."

3. Protection from adversaries

> Look upon my enemies, for they are many; and they hate me with violent hatred. Guard my soul and deliver me; do not let me be ashamed, for I take refuge in Thee. Let integrity and uprightness preserve me, for I wait for Thee. (Psalm 25:19–21)

For reasons unknown to us, people sometimes seek to hurt us. They seem to go out of their way to color information about us so they can inflict harm. David said it's all right to pray every day for God's deliverance from people like that. We need to pray for deliverance from our personal adversaries.

> *Today is Friday and therefore, my thoughts are focused on the weekend and the ministry of the Word of God and Worship. Lord, You know that I am teaching this weekend on that adversary, the Devil. I am not unaware of his power, but I thank You that he is not Your opposite. He is a created being and cannot do anything to me or my family or to this family of God without Your permission. I pray today that You will defeat him in every way and cause me to have great victory as I study and prepare for this lesson on Sunday. Lord, I have today and most of the day tomorrow to get this manuscript written, and I want to be so careful and so clear tomorrow that no one will misunderstand my teaching. Help me to be sensitive to potential errors in my teaching so that I might be accurate, and give me the right application to end the message with I pray.*

4. Deliverance from poverty and need

Behold, the eye of the LORD is on those who fear Him, on those who hope for His lovingkindness, to deliver their soul from death, and to keep them alive in famine." (Psalm 33:18–19)

Perhaps you're going through some very serious trials in your life right now and you wonder how God is going to take care of you. Have you prayed for God to deliver you? Pray for Him to do for you what He did for so many in the Bible. God still delivers!

I talk with Christian people all the time who are in the midst of awful trials. When I ask them, "Have you ever asked God pointedly, specifically, naming the details of this situation, to help you and deliver you?" they often admit they've prayed in general, but not specifically. If you're in the lion's den, you need to pray about the lion! If you're in the fire, you need to pray about the flames! David encourages us by his example to pray about human problems like poverty and violence.

5. Deliverance from fear

I sought the LORD, and He answered me, and delivered me from all my fears. (Psalm 34:4)

Have you ever had a fear day? I have. Sometimes, suddenly and out of nowhere, the spirit of fear grips my heart and I have to drop everything, leave my office, and go to a place I know by a lake. I walk and tell God about my fear, asking Him to deliver me from it.

Fear is paralyzing. Fear can keep us from doing the things God wants us to do. Fear can bring our minds to the end of a road we might not yet even be on. When I was in the midst of cancer treatments, people would sometimes come up to me at church and tell me about someone in their family who had the same thing I did. They'd proceed to tell me every trial that happened to that person. Maybe they were trying to relate to what I was experiencing, but I had to start walking away from those encounters. They made me afraid. Now when someone starts to tell me a cancer story, I stop them, put up my hands, and say, "Does this story have a happy ending?" If it doesn't, I tell them I don't want to deal with that fear today.

Do you have any fears today? Have you asked God to deliver you from them? Have you ever admitted, "Lord, I'm afraid! I don't like to be afraid. This thing has got me." Many of us have spent our whole lives building a relationship with God, but when Satan uses fear against us, he can take away our joy of walking with God. That's why Jesus tells us to pray every day, "Lord, deliver me from evil, including *all* my fear."

I think God is pleased when we come to Him in this way. We are saying, "If I could deliver myself, I wouldn't be asking You, Lord. But I know I can't, so please deliver me." God delights to hear that prayer from His children. Therefore Jesus taught us to pray: "God, this situation is beyond me. I can't cope with it. But You can. Please extend Your hand, and by your power, help me and deliver me."

DELIVER US FROM EVIL AND LEAD US HOME

Paul's swan song, his last will and testament, is recorded in 2 Timothy. The old apostle had suffered some severe hardships, including being brought to trial for his supposed crimes. These were his words in the last book to emerge from his pen before he died:

> But the Lord stood with me, and strengthened me, in order that through me the proclamation might be fully accomplished, and that all the Gentiles might hear; and I was delivered out of the lion's mouth. The Lord will deliver me from every evil deed, and will bring me safely to His heavenly kingdom; to Him be the glory forever and ever. Amen. (2 Timothy 4:17–18)

Don't forget this man's circumstances. He was in chains in a filthy Roman dungeon, waiting on death row. Two men named Phygelus and Hermogenes had abandoned him. Two other men named Hymenaeus and Philetus had become heretics. Alexander the coppersmith had vigorously opposed his message, prompting other believers to keep their mouths shut. Demas had deserted him. Crescens had left him. So had Titus. Tychicus was gone. Only Luke remained with him.

This was the moment of the apostle's greatest trial. When death stares you in the face, the temptation is strong to save your neck by renouncing your faith. Paul faced that test, and passed. Despite all his problems and the imminent execution he faced, Paul declared that God alone always stood with him. Everyone else had fled, but the Lord stood by him and delivered him. "I was delivered out of the lion's mouth," he wrote, then added for good measure, "The Lord will deliver me from every evil deed."

We read that last sentence and wonder, *How could he say that?* He knew he was about to die; he had just written, "I am already being poured out as a drink offering, and the time of my departure has come" (2 Timothy 4:6). Yet he could say that God would deliver him from every evil work and bring him safely to His heavenly kingdom.

How could he say such a thing? I'll tell you how. He knew he was on his way to heaven, and to his mind anything that got him safely there could never be called an "evil work." What was the worst thing the Romans could do to him? Pack him off to Paradise! He knew that is how God would deliver him.

We don't know if Paul prayed in his last moments, "Do not lead us into temptation, but deliver us from evil," but we do know one thing: He lived out the truth of those words. That truth kept him confident and expectant right to the very end. And it can do the same for us.

Chapter Ten

ENDING WHERE
WE BEGAN

"For Thine is the kingdom, and the power, and the glory, forever. Amen."

D r. A. J. Gordon of Gordon College and Gordon Conwell Divinity School had a dream that changed his life. It happened like this:

One Saturday night, Dr. Gordon, worn-out from working on Sunday's sermon, fell asleep and began to dream. He dreamt he was in the pulpit when a stranger came in and sat down. Gordon saw everything around the man with surreal clarity, even the pew number. But he could not see the man's face. He did remember, however, that the face wore a serious look, like a person who had great sorrow—and that it gave to him the most respectful attention. As he preached, he could not take his eyes off of the man. The man held his gaze rather than Gordon his.

The service over, Dr. Gordon tried to reach him through the crowded aisle, but the man was gone. Approaching the man who had sat beside the stranger, he asked who he was. Then came the laconic reply, "It was Jesus of Nazareth." Gordon chastised him for letting Jesus go, but the man replied nonchalantly,

"Oh, do not be troubled. He has been here today, and no doubt will come again."[1]

Gordon described this dream in one of his books, recording his shock and subsequent self-examination:

> One thought…lingered in my mind with something of comfort and more of awe. *"He has been here today, and no doubt will come again"*; and mentally repeating these words as one regretfully meditating on a vanished vision, I awoke and it was a dream. No, it was not a dream. It was a vision of the deepest reality, a miniature of actual ministry.[2]

The dream had a historic impact on this man's life. It gave him a profound sense of the presence of Christ and brought such blessing to his church that it ultimately spurred the foundation of Gordon College.

JESUS IS AMONG US

One cannot help but wonder what would happen today if *we* had such an awesome awareness of Christ's presence in our lives and churches!

Do we recognize that when we meet for worship, Christ is in our midst? I do not know which seat He chooses to occupy, but He is among us. When we come to God personally with our prayers, He is there, close by. He is not a far-off God; He is at hand. He has promised never to leave us nor forsake us. He is there when we pray to Him in the morning and before we pillow our head at night. He is the last One to know our thoughts at the end of the day and the first One to greet us in the morning. When we draw near to God, says the Scripture, He draws near to us (James 4:8).

The Bible says that God inhabits the praise of His people (Psalm 22:3, KJV). We sense His presence when we worship Him, for He manifests Himself when we praise Him. There is nothing in all of the world that will help us to understand and sense and feel the presence of God more than when we worship and praise Him. Therefore it should not surprise us to see that the pattern of prayer our Lord taught His disciples begins and ends with praise.

> *I had a wonderful time of prayer as I walked in the warehouse and rejoiced in the knowledge I have of my wonderful Savior. What a Savior! As I read today from Matthew about his stilling of the storms, multiplying of the loaves, healing of the sick, and raising of the dead, I was struck by this simple thought: this is my Savior—my Jesus. I know Him, and He knows me, which is even more marvelous and wonderful. How great it is to worship such a One!*

FROM GLORY TO GLORY

The Lord's Prayer ends as it began. We began with "hallowed be Thy name" and we end with "thine is the glory." We began with "Thy kingdom come" and end with "Thine is the kingdom." We began with "Thy will be done" and we end with "Thine is the power." We began with "on earth as it is in heaven" and we end with "forever and ever."

The last chord of our Lord's prayer brings us to the very mountain peak of praise and focuses our hearts and minds on the greatness and majesty of God. If we fail to end here, we will be left with more of a sense of our problems than with a hope of their solution. To prevent us from getting stuck, Jesus taught us a kind of "psychology of prayer." He taught us the right place to begin (honoring the name of God) and the proper way to end (praising God for His sovereignty and glory).

The doxology of the Lord's Prayer presents four major truths about God. Why these four? Our Lord could have chosen many others. But the more I study His prayer, the more I believe that these four realities are the ones we most desperately need to remember as we live and pray in a fallen world.

GOD IS SOVEREIGN

"Thine is the kingdom," Jesus prayed. The greatest exhibition of God's sovereignty (or control) is His anointing of His own Son to be king of this world. Scattered throughout the Bible are dozens of reminders that Jesus Christ is king. Here are just a handful:

He is King of heaven (Daniel 4:37).

He is King of the Jews (Matthew 2:2).

He is King of Israel (John 1:49).

He is King of the ages (1 Timothy 1:17).

He is King of glory (Psalm 24:7).

He is King of the saints (Revelation 15:3, KJV).

He is King of kings (1 Timothy 6:15).

He is the Prince of the kings of the earth (Revelation 1:5, KJV).

Jesus is King! The pagan ruler Nebuchadnezzar discovered that the hard way. When in his pride and arrogance he lifted himself above every authority, God took away his mind and for seven years forced him to eat hay like an ox. At the end of that time God had mercy on the king and restored to him not only his sanity, but also his kingdom. Nebuchadnezzar responded by saying, "I blessed the Most High and praised and honored Him who lives forever; For His dominion is an everlasting dominion, and His kingdom endures from generation to generation. And all the inhabitants of the earth are accounted as nothing, but He does according to His will in the host of heaven and among the inhabitants of earth; and no one can ward off His hand or say to Him, 'What hast Thou done?'" (Daniel 4:34, 35).

Another ruler many centuries later would learn the same lesson. After Napoleon Bonaparte was for the last time toppled from his European empire and forced to spend his last days in exile on the island of St. Helena, he wrote these moving words:

I die before my time and my body shall be given back to the earth and devoured by worms. What an abysmal gulf between my deep miseries and the eternal kingdom of Christ! I marvel that whereas the ambitious dreams of myself and Alexander and of Caesar should have vanished into thin air, a Judean peasant, Jesus, should be able to stretch his hands across the centuries, and control the destinies of men and nations.[3]

Jesus is King of kings and Lord of lords. You might think, *Well, it doesn't seem like He's doing a very good job of controlling things right now.* But we must remember that He has allowed Satan, for a time, to run most things in this world. The situation may look chaotic now, but one of these days Jesus will rule over His kingdom and there will be no dissonance in that reign. He will be absolutely and completely in control. Satan and his hosts will trouble us no more, for they will be cast into eternal fire. Everything will happen at the proper time, just as Scripture has prophesied. As Paul writes:

But now Christ has been raised from the dead, the first fruits of those who are asleep. For since by a man came death, by a man also came the resurrection of the dead. For as in Adam all die, so also in Christ all shall be made alive.

But each in his own order: Christ the first fruits, after that those who are Christ's at His coming, then comes the end, when He delivers up the kingdom to the God and Father, when He has abolished all rule and all authority and power. For He must reign until He has put all His enemies under His feet. The last enemy that will be abolished is death. For "He has put all things in subjection under His feet."

But when He says, "All things are put in subjection," it is evident that He is excepted who put all things in subjection to Him.

And when all things are subjected to Him, then the Son Himself also will be subjected to the One who subjected all things to Him, that God may be all in all. (1 Corinthians 15:20–28)

God really is the absolute Sovereign of the universe. When we understand that and believe that and act upon it, we are empowered to live our Christian lives in a way that attracts the interest of unbelievers. "Thine is the kingdom," prayed Jesus. God is sovereign. Praise His name!

GOD IS POWERFUL

God is not an absentee Ruler who sits at His controls and pulls switches and punches buttons to make people and events dance like marionettes. Our God is a hands-on God. "Thine is the kingdom *and the power*," Jesus said. God is actively involved every day in energizing this world and keeping it working. And He knows everything—the front from the back, the middle to the outside. He knows all that's going on and He never makes a mistake. Sometimes we forget that.

Several years ago, during a time of discouragement in my life, someone gave me this little poem:

My Father's way may twist and turn,
    My heart may throb and ache,
But in my soul I'm glad I know,
    He maketh no mistake.

My cherished plans may go astray,
    My hopes may fade away,
But still I'll trust my Lord to lead
    For He doth know the way.

Though night be dark and it may seem
    The day will never break;

I'll pin my faith, my all in Him,
>   He maketh no mistake.

There's so much now I cannot see,
>   My eyesight's far too dim;
But come what may, I'll simply trust
>   And leave it all to Him.

For by and by the mist will lift
>   And plain it all He'll make,
Through all the way, though dark to me,
>   He maketh no mistake.[4]

Nothing is too difficult for God. When Abraham was an old man (and according to Paul, "as good as dead," Romans 4:19), God said to him, "I will make you the father of a multitude of nations" (Genesis 17:5). Abraham initially laughed at the idea, but Paul says "with respect to the promise of God, he did not waver in unbelief, but grew strong in faith, giving glory to God, and being fully assured that what He had promised, He was able also to perform. Therefore also it was reckoned to him as righteousness" (Romans 4:20–22). Out of a promise which seemed so impossible came the great nation of the Jewish people. When such a promise is backed up with infinite power, it's a good idea to believe the Promise Giver!

One time Jesus told His disciples that it was easier for a camel to pass through the eye of a needle than for a rich man to enter heaven. The disciples were astonished because they equated physical blessings with divine favor. So they asked Jesus, "Then who can be saved?" Jesus replied, "With men this is impossible, but with God all things are possible" (Matthew 19:25, 26). Some of us have loved ones for whom we've been praying and we've wondered if it's possible for God to change them. Is it? Absolutely! There is no one so lost and so far from God that His divine power can't reach into that person's heart and transform him or her, for *His is the power*.

Perhaps you have heard about the amazing changes that have happened in the past few years within one of the nation's most notorious cults. The Worldwide Church of God, begun in the early 1930s by the late Herbert W. Armstrong, delighted in calling all other groups but itself "harlot daughters." The church was rigidly controlled from the top and was known for extreme legalism, for wild prophecies about the return of Christ that never came true, for teaching that the United States and Great Britain were actually the ten lost tribes of Israel, for insisting that members tithe up to thirty percent of their incomes, for declaring that Sunday worship was desperate sin, and on and on. At its height, this group's twin publicity vehicles—the slick magazine *The Plain Truth* and its equally slick television program "The World Tomorrow"—reached an audience of millions every week. To the evangelical world, the Worldwide Church of God looked like an impregnable fortress dedicated to vilifying the historic Christian faith.

What most of us did not see was a group of dedicated Christians who were praying for this group and its leaders. These faithful believers paid no attention to those who said no cult in history had ever turned its back on its heretical teachings to enter the Christian mainstream. They prayed anyway, for ten, twenty, thirty, forty or more years. They prayed that the light of the true gospel might dawn in the hearts of many members of this group and that God would use His Word to bring them into His family. They prayed that He would do a miracle.

And you know what? He did!

Starting in about 1990 and continuing to the present day, the Worldwide Church of God has made profound changes in its teaching and practice. Its leaders have apologized for their past attacks on other churches. They have officially renounced their former cultic theology and have embraced the historic Christian faith as taught in the Bible and affirmed by the ancient church creeds. Oh, they have paid a hefty price for doing so—their church's membership has declined in those few years by more than half, its income has dropped even more, and the WCG leadership continues to receive angry and even threatening letters from disgruntled former members. Yet "the changes," as they are called in the church, are here to stay. God has done a mighty, unexpected work in their midst, and they have no desire to return to bondage. It is the first time in history a cult has made such a 180-degree shift.

God is powerful beyond our imaginations! It is not without reason that Paul wrote of our Lord, "Now to Him who is able to do exceeding abundantly beyond all that we ask or think, according to the power that works within us, to Him be the glory in the church and in Christ Jesus to all generations forever and ever. Amen" (Ephesians 3:20–21).

After I've asked God for some pretty big things, I'm glad to end my prayer with the reminder that God is supremely powerful. The throne in heaven is not empty. God is there, seated and in control. He can do whatever He determines to do. He said a word and the worlds were made. He spoke and the moon and stars were flung into space. He is an awesome, almighty God. And my prayer links me to Him! Talk about power!

You, too, can be linked to that kind of power...if you want to be. You don't have to get up every morning and psych yourself up for it, either, because God's power is always there. You just have to plug in.

GOD IS MAJESTIC

"For Thine is...the glory," Jesus prayed. What is glory?

> Glory is what you see when you peer out of an airplane at thirty thousand feet and are swept away by the bright glow of an orange and pink and red and purple sunset flaming its brilliance behind the snow-capped peaks of a majestic mountain range. Glory is beauty. Glory is splendor. Glory is magnificence. Glory is all that is worthy of praise and honor and shouts of great joy.

And it is glory that our Father in heaven plans to shower upon us in downpours that will never cease.[5]

Our God is a God of glory. The primary word for "glory" in the Old Testament is *kabod*, which appears two hundred times. In the New International Version, this term is translated "glory" some one hundred twenty times, "honor" thirty-three times, "splendor" six times, and "pomp" three times. The term is derived from a related word that literally means "to be heavy," recalling C.S. Lewis' famous book *The Weight of Glory*. Bible scholars have described the term like this:

Over against the transience of human and earthly glory stands the unchanging beauty of the manifest God (Psalm 145:5). In this sense the noun *kabod* takes on its most unusual and distinctive meaning. Forty-five times this form of the root relates to a visible manifestation of God and whenever "the glory of God" is mentioned this usage must be taken account of. Its force is so compelling that it remolds the meaning of *doxa* from an opinion of men in the Greek classics to something absolutely objective in the [Septuagint] and [New Testament]....

The several references which speak of God's glory filling the earth and/or becoming evident are instructive. On the one hand they quite legitimately refer to that reputation for greatness which God alone deserves, not only because of his natural position as king, but because of his unsurpassed activity as deliverer and saviour. However...something more is intended here. It is not merely God's reputation which fills the earth, but it is the very reality of his presence. And his desire is that all persons may gladly recognize and own this....

But nowhere is the reality and the splendor of his presence and his character seen as in his son (Isaiah 4:2). Here the near-blinding quality of his glory is fully portrayed, "We beheld his glory, the glory as of the only son of the Father, full of grace and truth" (John 1:14; cf. 17:1–5). Through him and through his presence in the church, God's glory is indeed filling the earth.[6]

As mentioned in the first paragraph of this quote, the primary word for "glory" in the New Testament is *doxa*, from which we get our word "doxology." The word is usually translated "glory" and occasionally as "splendor," "honor," "brilliance" or "majesty."

But whatever word is used to translate the original terms, the idea is the same in both testaments. God is a God of glory, of majesty, of splendor, of beauty and honor and astonishing brilliance. That is why Paul calls Him "the blessed and only Sovereign, the King of kings and Lord of lords; who alone possesses immortality and dwells in unapproachable light; whom no man has seen or can see. To Him be honor and eternal dominion! Amen" (1 Timothy 6:15–16).

> *Lord, You are omniscient. You know what will happen tomorrow and the day after that. You see eternity and You know how all these things fit into Your plan! I can only see today and only feel the pain of this moment. I have no concept of eternity except to know You are eternal. Lord, You know what You are doing with me—I do not! I must trust Your judgment and Your all-knowing wisdom to show me what to do every moment of each day. If I thought You did not know as I do not know, I would really have reason for fear and despair.*

The Bible says that God covers Himself with light as with a garment (Psalm 104:2, NIV). In the same way you and I put on our clothes every day, God clothes Himself with sunbeams. He is light, "and in Him there is no darkness at all" (1 John 1:5). When we pray, "Thine is the glory," we remind ourselves that the One to whom we pray is the almighty God, the God of glory whose brilliance fills the earth. If for one moment our God should remove Himself from this world, all would be darkness.

So bright is this divine illumination that the Bible tells us when we're in heaven, there will be no need for a sun by day or a moon by night, for the Lamb Himself shall be the light (Revelation 21:23). The Lord Jesus will illuminate the whole universe!

Remember that the next time you pray, "Thine is...the glory." Remember all that is wrapped up in that remarkable term. And then worship the God of glory whose majesty fills the universe with brilliant, blazing light.

GOD IS ETERNAL

Think for a moment about your house, however big or small it might be. You inhabit your house. When you walk inside, you see walls which shape the space you call home. The Bible says that God lives in a house called eternity. Isaiah calls God "the High and Lofty One Who inhabits eternity" (Isaiah 57:15, NKJV). And how big is eternity? As far back as you can think, and then further back than you can imagine, and then further back than imagination has any potential to dream. Eternity is forever. There never was a time when it was not. And how far into the future does it reach? On and on and on.... There never will be a time when it ceases to be. Our God is eternal.

That's what Jesus meant when He spoke the last little word of this sentence, "forever." The word is not unimportant; it's much more than a convenient way to end the prayer. "Forever" is an awesome word and it's the perfect end to this perfect prayer. But what good is this to us?

I stood with God on the edge of the world. My hand was in his hand. I looked down the road of the past as it stretched away in the dim distance until it was shrouded in the mists of time. I knew it had no beginning. A little chill wind of fear blew about my head, and God said, "Are you afraid?"

And I said, "Yes, I am afraid because I cannot understand how there can be no beginning."

So God said, "Let us turn and face the other way."

And I looked into glory and my heart rejoiced with joy unspeakable. Then my mind went ahead a billion billion years, and I knew there would be no end. And again, that little chill wind of fear began to blow. God said, "Are you afraid?"

And I answered, "I am afraid a little because I cannot understand how there can be no end."

God asked me tenderly, "Are you afraid now, here, today, with your hand in mine?"

And I looked at him and smiled and replied, "O my Father, no."

And God said, "Every day in eternity will be today."[7]

Every day in eternity will be today! Are you happy with the way it is with God and you right now? Has He provided for you? You got up this morning, took some nourishment, got dressed, and began your day. Right now we're thinking of all these good things about the Lord. Are you OK with God right now? Right now, at this moment? With God, every day is today. He's eternal.

Never think He sits up in heaven, wringing His hands over what might happen to you tomorrow or the next day. God sees the end from the beginning. We have nothing to fear from the future, for every day with God is today. And He can be trusted. We know that because of His unblemished history of faithfulness. What a legacy! The Bible says it this way: "Jesus Christ is the same yesterday and today, yes and forever" (Hebrews 13:8). He's never in a bad mood. No day is any better than today for you to ask

Him your question. He won't change His mind tomorrow. You can bring anything to God this very moment, for He lives in the eternal now.

When we finish praying the doxology of the Lord's Prayer, we're ready to go. We don't have to worry about what's going to happen today because God is in control. "Thine is the kingdom." We don't have to concern ourselves with how we're going to get through a particular challenge because God says, "I can do it! Just trust me. Mine is the power." All we need to remember is who He is and what He promises. "Mine is the glory." And we can relax and trust in His provision, because He never changes. He is the same good God "forever."

THINK ABOUT IT

We've spent the past several chapters carefully thinking through each critical part of the prayer Jesus taught His disciples in response to their request, "Lord, teach us to pray." Perhaps now would be a good time once more to review the whole prayer as a unit:

> Our Father who art in heaven
> Hallowed be Thy name.
> Thy kingdom come.
> Thy will be done,
> On earth as it is in heaven.
> Give us this day our daily bread.
> And forgive us our debts, as we also have forgiven our debtors.
> And do not lead us into temptation, but deliver us from evil.
> For Thine is the kingdom, and the power, and the glory, forever.
> Amen.

This is a marvel of a prayer, chock full of deep theology, divine wisdom, and great encouragement. Yet it also should cause us to ask some probing questions of ourselves. As one author has written:

Can you say "our" if your religion has no room for others and their needs? Can you say "Father" if you have not been born again and adopted as His child through the blood of Christ shed for your sin? Can you say "Who art in heaven" if all your interests and pursuits are on earth? Can you say "hallowed be Thy name" if the One who is called by that name is not holy to you? Can you say "Thy kingdom come" if you are unwilling to give up your independence and accept the righteous reign of God? Can you say "Thy will be done" if you're unwilling or resentful of having to relinquish your own agenda? Can you say "on earth as it is in heaven" if you're not truly ready to give yourself to His service here and now?

Can you say "give us this day our daily bread" without expending honest effort for it, or by ignoring the needs of your fellow man? Can you say "forgive us our debts as we forgive our debtors" if you continue to hold a grudge against someone? Can you say "lead us not into temptation" if you deliberately choose to remain in a situation where you're going to be tempted? Can you say "deliver us from evil" if you're not prepared to fight in the spiritual realm with the weapon of prayer? Can you say "Thine is the kingdom" if you don't give the King the disciplined obedience of a loyal subject? Can you say "Thine is the power" if you fear what your friends and neighbors may say or do? Can you say "Thine is the glory" if you're seeking your own glory first? Can you say "forever" if you're full of anxiety about the here and now? Can you say "amen" if you don't honestly mean, "Cost what it may, this is my prayer"?[8]

How did you do on this little quiz? While I'm quite sure none of us got a perfect score—I know I didn't—it's a good reminder of the goal we must keep in view. The Lord's Prayer is not merely a beautiful collection of words and cherished syllables, it's a model for us to follow in our prayer lives. It wasn't created to make us feel guilty or unworthy, but to show us the proper and most effective way to enter the very throne room of God Almighty. Incredible as it may seem, God is waiting to hear from us. He wants us to come boldly into His presence. And this prayer shows us the way.

LET'S GET ON THE TRACK

When people ask South Korean pastor Cho how he prays for so many hours every day, he says he just gets on the prayer track in the morning and starts running laps. The track he's talking about is the Lord's Prayer— the pattern prayer our Lord taught His disciples.[9]

We're to start our prayers with praise: "Our Father in heaven, hallowed be Your name." If left to us, our praying would both start and end with ourselves. Our natural self-centeredness has no boundaries. Many Christians have never prayed the way God taught them because as soon as they say, "Our heavenly Father," they start talking about all the things they need and all the things they want. There's nothing wrong with sensing our need, but there is something wrong with rushing into the presence of God with our litany of requests before we even recognize His greatness and honor His name. If we don't start our prayers by praising His name, we'll focus on our many problems instead of on the greatness of God—and we'll be in worse shape when we get done praying than we were before we started.

After we've praised God, we're to think through our priorities: "God, here's my life. I think I know what I want, but if it's not what You want, then I don't want it. I've lived long enough to know that You know more about what's good for me than I do, and Your priorities need to be my priorities. I want You to be sovereign over my life as a person, sovereign over my marriage as a partner, sovereign over my children as a parent, sovereign over my workplace as a provider, and sovereign over everything I do. 'Thy kingdom come, Thy will be done on earth as it is in heaven.'"

Once we've praised God and given our priorities to Him to direct, we come to our own needs. As we continue to run around the prayer track, we ask, "Give us this day our daily bread." We're to ask and it will be given to us, seek and we will find, knock and it will be opened to us. "But doesn't God already know about my needs?" someone asks. Sure He does. So why do we have to ask Him to meet those needs? Because He tells us to. He tells us to ask Him for what we need. Does that mean God will give us every little thing we want? No. He hasn't promised to do that. He's promised to give us the things we *need*—and only for today. God hasn't promised to fulfill our every fantasy. We may pray for a Cadillac, but it may be His will for us to drive a Hyundai. And there's nothing wrong with that! A Hyundai gets us where we're going as well as a Cadillac can. If God gives us a Hyundai when we pray for a Cadillac, He's done what He said He would do. So let's not worry. God will provide for us if we bring our priorities in line with His and turn over our needs to His care.

As we keep running around the track of the Lord's Prayer we come to "Forgive us our debts as we forgive our debtors." If we have a relationship a bit out of sync when we start praying this part, God will bring it to our frontal lobes and we'll have to deal with it. God requires us to be men and women of forgiveness. We're to forgive *because* we have been forgiven. We're to forgive *just as* we have been forgiven. We're to forgive *before we need to be* forgiven. And we're to forgive *always*. It's always our turn. Next time you have a late-night spat with your spouse and you're lying on opposite sides of the bed thinking, *Well, the last time this happened, I was the one who took the initiative to get it right*, just do it again! Keep on initiating, because that's what the Bible says. It's always our turn.

The next bend in the track calls for us to pray for God's protection: "Lead us not into temptation but deliver us from evil." What would happen to us if we said this prayer every day? How much might we be protected from life's calamities if we just prayed that God would carry us through the day without allowing us to yield to temptation? We're all solution-oriented people. We run into a problem and before we stop to ask God about it, we jump in and get it all sorted out. Then we go our way, worrying and fretting about what might happen. If only we would stop and say, "God, You take control. You do what you need to do, and I'll follow. I may not understand what's going on, but I know it's in Your hands and Your control. You be the one in charge. You deliver me."

Then, when we've finished making our requests and we're almost around the track, we go back to praise again. Praise seals every prayer we offer. As we proclaim, "Thine is the kingdom and the power and the glory forever," we are reminded that God is sovereign, that He is powerful, that He is majestic, and that He is eternal.

And who cannot say "Amen" to that?

> Lord, I end where I began—praising You and giving You the glory for all that You have done and for all that You mean in my life today! You are my God, and I am delighted to be Your son and Your minister! I praise Your name for Your goodness to me, and Your love for my family, and for Your kindness to all around me. I love You today, Lord, and I seek to honor You with my life this day. Amen!

Part Three

SEE HOW IT GLITTERS

Chapter Eleven

THE GREATEST PRAYER EVER OFFERED

I f one hundred people were asked how the Lord's Prayer starts, at least ninety-nine would say, "Our Father which art in heaven." And they would be wrong.

When the disciples asked Jesus to teach them how to pray, He responded with a model prayer, usually called the Lord's Prayer. But this cannot be the *Lord's* prayer, for the sinless Son of God never had any need to pray, "forgive me My debts." Jesus never asked for forgiveness, for the simple reason that He never sinned. What we normally call the Lord's Prayer would much more accurately be called the Disciples' Prayer.

If you want the *real* Lord's Prayer, you have to turn to John 17. This is the High Priestly prayer of the Lord Jesus. I am not exaggerating when I say it may be the greatest chapter in the Bible.

A PRAYER FOR THE AGES

I have studied this remarkable prayer for many years and every time I pick up an exposition or a book or a commentary about it, I read again how it has impacted great men of God.

For instance, Bishop J.C. Ryle said of this passage of Scripture, "The chapter we now have open to us is the most remarkable chapter in the

Bible. It stands alone, and there is none other like it." The Reformer Philip Melancthon wrote, "There is no voice which has ever been heard, either in heaven or in earth, more exalted, more holy, more fruitful, more sublime than the prayer offered up by the Son to God himself." And William Kelly, another great expositor of days past, wrote that "John 17 is a chapter which one may perhaps characterize truly as unequaled for depth and scope in all of the Scriptures."

Powerful leaders throughout church history—Martin Luther, John Calvin, Jonathan Edwards, Charles Spurgeon, and many more—have reserved their highest accolades for John 17. There is ample reason for their praise.

None of the other 650 prayers recorded in the Bible come close to matching the excellencies of the one found in John 17. The Gospels record nineteen occasions on which Jesus prayed, but this is the only long prayer of Jesus we have and the only one which gives us the substance of what He prayed. In the twenty-six verses of John 17, the Holy Spirit has been pleased to record Jesus' entire prayer in the upper room. In this prayer we see the blessed Son of God praying to the Father—not for a city, not for a nation, but for the whole world. He is interceding before the Father on behalf of His own.

> First of all, Lord Jesus, I want to express my deep gratitude that You are the High Priest of my life. And as I have read in Hebrews today, I am the recipient of all of your love and care because You came into the world to be one of us. In all things, You were made like unto the brethren that You might be a merciful and faithful High Priest to me! I take great encouragement from the fact that everything I am facing and will ever face You have already faced down. As I make my list of concerns in just a few moments, help me to remember that the One to whom I am bringing these things has already been there and done that!

Someone has written that as you come to John 17, it's as if the veil has been drawn aside and you are allowed to walk into the Holy of Holies with the High Priest Himself. Therefore as we approach the secret place of the tabernacle of the Most High—as we come to John 17—we do well to take our shoes off, spiritually speaking, and remember that we are walking on holy ground.

LISTENING IN TO HEAVEN'S CONVERSATION

We cannot read John 17 without recognizing it as communication between members of the Trinity. Here is God the Son talking to God the Father— and by the grace of God the Holy Spirit, we are privileged to listen in!

Have you ever wondered what goes on "up there"? Have you ever thought how fascinating it would be to tune in to heavenly conversations between the members of the Trinity? What do they talk about? What do they say? What goes on? We are favored in John 17 to hear part of such a dialogue.

It is a great gift...but even so, some may question the value of this gift. Why should we study this prayer? What difference will it make to the way we live? So what if we're allowed to hear Jesus pray—how is it going to change us? How is examining this prayer going to help us? Before we go any further, let me suggest two reasons why we ought to spend time meditating on this extraordinary prayer.

1. Studying this prayer reveals Christ's present work for us

When most of us study the life of Christ and read about His life and ministry and miracles, we get all excited about His crucifixion, death, and resurrection. Sometimes we even go a little further and ponder His ascension. But most of the time we stop there. It's almost as if we think Jesus Christ was put on hold for a few thousand years until the Second Coming. But John 17 gives us a profound appreciation for the continuing, ongoing ministry of Jesus Christ on our behalf. *Right now* in heaven

He is interceding for us and representing our interests before the Father. How encouraging this is!

Isn't it interesting that Jesus prayed out loud in front of His disciples so that they would be able to hear what He said? He did that on purpose. He did it so they would know He was committed to using all of His influence with the Father on their behalf. He wanted His disciples to know that as He prayed, He was representing them to the Sovereign of the Universe. He wanted them to hear Him say to His Father, "On My behalf and for My sake, will You do these things for My disciples?" He wanted His followers to know He would do everything in His power to meet their needs. He wanted them to know they would always have a wonderful and special place in His heart. It was this prayer, which they overheard, that proved how precious they were to Him.

A paraphrase of John 17:13 says, "These are the prayers which in heaven I will never cease to make before God, but I make them now in the world in your hearing so that you will know that I am going to be always promoting your welfare in heaven. When you know this, you will be partakers of My joy." Jesus wanted His disciples to know what He was doing to promote their welfare as He sat at the right hand of the Father in heaven, making intercession for them.

A song titled "Someone is Praying for You" has often been performed in our church. Occasionally the soloist has received notes from listeners questioning the song's validity. One of these notes asked, "How can you boldly stand up and sing that song to the whole congregation when there might be someone out there for whom nobody is praying? How do you know someone is praying for everybody who hears that song?"

The soloists don't need to worry about the accuracy of their song, for John 17 makes it clear that "Somebody" *is* praying for all of us! We never go without Someone making intercession for us, for that is what Jesus is doing on our behalf right now. We know this not only from John 17, but also from passages such as these:

Hence, also, He [Christ] is able to save forever those who draw near to God through Him, since He always lives to make intercession for them (Hebrews 7:25).

Who is the one who condemns? Christ Jesus is He who died, yes, rather who was raised, who is at the right hand of God, who also intercedes for us (Romans 8:34).

For Christ did not enter a holy place made with hands, a mere copy of the true one, but into heaven itself, now to appear in the presence of God for us (Hebrews 9:24).

Every time you and I pray, Jesus Christ takes our prayers and interprets them perfectly so that they come to God the Father in exactly the right way and accomplish everything they need to. Even when we're not praying, even when we're unconscious, the Bible says that Jesus is making intercession for us, representing our case to the Father, praying on our behalf.

2. Studying this prayer reveals Christ's perfect will for us

One sure way to increase stress is to try to operate from multiple agendas. When we try to go in several directions at once, our stress level is bound to skyrocket. We know as Christians that the only agenda that counts is the Lord's; we are called to follow Him alone. That's easy enough to say, but the crucial question is, what is *on* the Lord's agenda? What items appear on His list?

One of the best ways to discover what's really important to a person is to listen in on his or her prayers. If you could eavesdrop on someone's private prayers for two or three mornings in a row, you would be able to tell what was on that person's heart. When we pray, we unburden our souls. We tell God everything that's happening in our lives, everything that concerns us. We pray for our families, for our needs, for our churches, for our friends and communities. We pray for our future and our health and our deepest desires. If we could listen in while someone prayed, we would know what was on his or her agenda.

That is exactly our privilege in John 17. The Lord has enabled us to tune our ear to His praying, and when we finish listening to Him pray, we will know what is on His agenda. That is so exciting! Knowing His agenda will enable us to sort out some things, to get our priorities reorganized. When we listen to Jesus pray in John 17, we discover that only four things are at the top of His priority list. They're simple things, and yet we are to give our lives to them.

> *We are not commanded to achieve perfection in terms of the things above, but we are commanded to keep on seeking the things above. Lord, I know that is my heart in this matter—to be a seeker of things above! To strive after You, to want to know You and grow in my knowledge of You day by day! I will never arrive completely this side of heaven, but I will keep seeking and striving to know You, and with Paul to say that my goal is "to know You and the fellowship of Your suffering and then to be made conformable unto Your death"!*

SIMPLE PRAYER, PROFOUND RAMIFICATIONS

Jesus' prayer is organized in three basic sections. In verses 1–5 we find Him praying for Himself; in verses 6–19 He prays for His disciples; and in verses 20–26 Jesus prays for His church. As we read John 17 and try to understand what is important to Jesus, what are the burdens on His heart? Four things stand out above all others.

1. That Jesus might be glorified

First on the heart of Jesus is that He might be glorified. John writes, "These things Jesus spoke; and lifting up His eyes to heaven, He said, 'Father, the hour has come; glorify Thy Son, that the Son may glorify Thee'" (verse 1). A few verses later Jesus says, "And now, glorify Thou Me together with Thyself, Father, with the glory which I had with Thee before the world was" (verse 5).

We are taught from the Word of God and from the church creeds that the chief end of man is to glorify God. As we read this prayer and see the heart of the Lord Jesus in it, we discover His intense desire that He be glorified with the same glory He displayed before He left heaven for earth. His request reminds us that our top priority must be to glorify our Lord. We would be wise to ask ourselves, why do we do what we do? What is our purpose behind our work, our play, our service, our relationships? John 17 reveals that the top item for us on Jesus' agenda is that we bring glory to Him.

And how do we do this? We do so by making sure our actions reflect well on our Savior. When people gain a taste of heaven by sampling the righteous deeds and attitudes we serve up, Jesus is glorified. Just the other day I heard of one such divine snack. An elderly woman in a small Minnesota town had just lost her husband to a long illness. Her neighbor, a Christian, took it upon himself to clear the snow choking her sidewalks. She didn't ask him to do it and he didn't wait for an invitation. He simply saw the need, he had the time and the snowblower, and he went to work. And right there, in the teeth of a frigid Minnesota winter, that woman got a whiff of heavenly cooking. And Jesus was glorified.

2. That Christians might be sanctified

In verse 11 Jesus says, "And I am no more in the world; and yet they themselves [Christians] are in the world, and I come to Thee. Holy Father, keep them in Thy name, the name which Thou hast given Me." Also note verse 15: "I do not ask Thee to take them out of the world, but to keep them from the evil one." Repeatedly throughout His prayer we find that the heartbeat of Jesus is for God's people to be sanctified.

Allow me to de-Christianize that word "sanctify." When I was growing up, people used to get up and testify, "I'm just thankful that I'm saved and sanctified." I didn't know what they meant. I found out later their testimonies were false. Some of them *weren't* sanctified, for the word "sanctified" means "to be holy." And these folks were anything but.

Isn't it interesting that at the heart of the Lord's High Priestly prayer is His desire that the people of God should be holy, righteous, sanctified, and set apart from the world?

If ever a prayer were needed in our world, it's this one. We have become so like the world and we've invited so much of the world into the church that it's hard to tell the difference between the two. A few years ago authors James Patterson and Peter Kim published a book titled, *The Day America Told the Truth: What People Really Believe About Everything that Really Matters.* Consider some of their startling conclusions:

> What is going on in congregations, parishes and synagogues across America? The news is good and bad.
>
> God is alive and well. But right now in America, fewer people are listening to what God has to say than ever before.
>
> Ninety percent of the people we questioned said that they believe in God. It would be the logical conclusion then to think that God is a meaningful factor in today's America. But we reached a different conclusion when we dug deeper with our questions.
>
> In every single region of the country, when we asked how people make up their minds on issues of right and wrong, we found that they simply do not turn to God or religion to help them decide about the seminal or moral issues of the day. For most people, religion plays no role in shaping their opinions on a long list of important public questions. This is true even for questions that seem closely related to religion: birth control, abortion, even teaching creationism and the role of women in the clergy. On not one of these questions did a majority of people

seek the guidance of religion in finding answers. Most people do not even know their church's position on the important issues.

...Only one in 10 of us believe in all of the Ten Commandments. Forty percent of us believe in five or fewer Commandments.

We have established ourselves as the authority on morality. We now choose which Commandments to believe and which ones not to believe. Clearly, the God of the 1990s in America is a distant and pale reflection of the God of our forefathers.[1]

I wish Patterson and Kim's conclusions were inaccurate, but they're not. The evidence is everywhere. Not too long ago a friend told me he spotted a car sporting a chrome "fish" symbol with the name "Jesus" inside it, a "dove" sign on the bumper and the name of a Christian college plastered on the rear windshield. Hanging from the rearview mirror inside the car was an air freshener in the form of a Playboy bunny.

Obviously, this is not what Jesus was praying for. The prayer and heartbeat of Jesus is that the church of Jesus Christ might be holy and sanctified. It's a prayer which we must echo with increasing urgency.

3. That the church might be unified

In verse 21 Jesus prayed, "that they may all be one; even as Thou, Father, art in Me, and I in Thee, that they also may be in Us." He says repeatedly in verses 21–23 that He desires His church to be unified. What does He mean?

I'm frequently asked, "Do you believe in the ecumenical movement?" I usually respond with a saying of C.S. Lewis: "There is no clever arrangement of rotten eggs that will ever make a good omelet." The ecumenical movement is a misguided, human attempt to take all organized churches—regardless of what any individual denomination believes— and force them together into some sort of outward unity. I don't believe in that, and neither does the Bible.

That's not what Jesus is talking about here. He doesn't have in mind ecumenical unity, but the spiritual unity of all true members of the body of Christ. The problem today is that Christians—genuine, blood-bought believers in the Risen Christ—can't get along with each other. We somehow lack unity among believers of like, precious faith. It's no longer a matter of whether the saved Baptists get along with the saved Methodists or the saved Presbyterians or the saved Lutherans. The saved Baptists don't even get along with the saved Baptists!

Perhaps you've heard how a couple of old church hymns have been rewritten to reflect this ungodly antagonism:

"Amazing grace, how sweet the sound
        that saved a wretch like you."

"The strife is o'er, the battle done
        the church has split and our side won."

I believe the Lord's heart is broken by what He sees. His prayer isn't being answered right now, because the body of Christ has chosen to fracture and fragment itself. It doesn't have to be that way.

Some time ago I spoke to a group of Christians in the Seattle area who had gathered to find biblical help for their families. On a Thursday, Friday and Saturday, I and some others ministered to some two thousand people from every kind of church imaginable, all of them committed to the historic Christian faith. For three days nobody asked about denominational affiliation. Nobody cared. We came together in our mutual faith in Christ to learn from the Word of God anything that would help us be better fathers and mothers and parents. We enjoyed a sweet oneness in Christ.

Something like that needs to happen on a much larger scale in the body of Christ if we're going to fulfill the prayer of Jesus. He wants us to be unified, not through some bogus organizational structure, but through our mutual faith and trust in Him. If God is our Father, then we're all brothers and sisters in Christ. And it's about time we started acting like it.

4. That the world might be evangelized

There's one last request, found in verse 18: "As Thou didst send Me into the world, I also have sent them into the world." Why did Jesus come into the world? Answer: To seek and to save that which was lost. And why are we sent into the world? Answer: To seek and to save that which is lost.

In the second half of verse 21 Jesus asked His Father that the church might be unified so "that the world may believe that Thou didst send Me." The Father had sent Jesus from heaven to earth to redeem a people for His very own. Jesus was now about to go to the cross to achieve that purpose. Just a few days after His resurrection, He would return to heaven, yet His mission to redeem the world would go on. The necessary sacrifice, Himself, already would have been made—but word about that sacrifice needed to be spread. How would that happen? Through the disciples. Jesus was saying, "Father, you sent Me out of heaven into this world and now I'm getting ready to come back to be with You. Just as You sent Me into this world, to represent You, so I'm sending the disciples into the world to be Your ambassadors."

Jesus' heartbeat was evangelism and missionary outreach. He had a passion that all men and women might be saved. That's what He prayed about in this remarkable prayer. So what does that mean to us? If we're going to operate on the agenda of Jesus, we will strive to discover and fulfill our part in the evangelization of the world. And what is that part? It varies for each of us, but all of us have a part, no matter what our age or gifts or backgrounds.

Not long before he died, Donald McGavran, the famed church growth expert, was speaking to a group of senior adults. At ninety-three years of age, he said, "Many people think their lives stop when they retire, that their real work has ended. When I retired at age sixty-eight, the most important work of my life began. Let me assure you, my friends, that your real life has begun and probably your most important contribution will be made in the coming years. But see to it that you deal with important matters. See to it that you deal with the church. See to it that you deal with bringing people to Christ."

So you're not a church growth expert? You're not an evangelist? Not many are. But if you're a Christian, you're an ambassador for God. Woodie W. White tells this story about how he came to faith:

> In the fall of 1953 I met a young woman at a soda fountain. At the time I was having severe difficulty with organized religion. She was an articulate and dedicated Christian. She knew how to talk about her faith. The more I railed against the Church, the more she talked about Jesus. The more I talked about the hypocrites in the Church, the more she talked about Jesus. The more I pointed to the failure of the Church, the more she talked about Jesus. She won. Praise God!
>
> Maybe we are using our evangelistic witness to talk about the wrong things. Perhaps we are giving answers to questions no one is asking. It may well be that people are looking for bread and we are giving a stone. The Good News is: Jesus is Lord! Whatever else may follow, and there is much, this is where the Story begins.[2]

Jesus has a passion for the salvation of men and women, boys and girls, a passion expressed in His High Priestly prayer. If we wish to operate on His agenda, we will see what part we can play in bringing people to Christ.

SOME PRACTICAL SUGGESTIONS

If the agenda of Jesus is our own agenda, we will strive for everything He prayed for in this prayer. Do you know what that would do for most of us? It would filter out a lot of things we're currently doing. We could quickly jettison a whole lot of excess baggage if we got back to the heartbeat of the Savior as expressed in this magnificent prayer.

May I make a suggestion? One way to align ourselves with the agenda of Christ is to bathe ourselves in His deepest concerns. And one of the best ways to do that is to meditate on His High Priestly prayer. The whole prayer takes only six minutes to read; I timed it. If you're a slow reader it might take eight minutes, but no more. Let me suggest that for the next thirty days, you read through this prayer once each day. That will take a little discipline on your part, but for six minutes a day, you can do it. Find some time, pick up whatever translation of the Scripture you like, and read John 17 every day for thirty days. If you do that, your life will change. I can almost guarantee that two practical things will happen when you spend extended time with this prayer.

First, you'll learn the crucial *place* of prayer in ministry. For four chapters prior to His High Priestly prayer, Jesus gave His disciples some concentrated instruction. When you finally arrive at John 17, you discover that almost every theme developed in the teaching of John 13–16 is repeated in the prayer of Jesus in John 17. It's almost as if Jesus is saying to us, "Teaching is not enough! Ministering is not enough! All teaching without prayer is like light without heat, and all ministry without bathing that ministry in prayer is just a perfunctory, ritual performance."

Could this explain why we have so much empty, dead ministry in our world? We're out there doing it, but without prayer to empower it. If Jesus Christ Himself taught and taught and taught and then prayed that truth into the hearts of His disciples, how can we do any less? Prayer is essential to all ministry. In fact, without it, ministry does not happen.

When I was in school at Dallas Theological Seminary, Dr. Howard Hendricks used to tell us, "You haven't taught if the students haven't learned." I heard that and I decided it was about time to quit. Do you know how hard it is to make students learn? You can't do it; it's supernatural. It's the Spirit of God who makes truth come alive in human hearts. And how does He do that? In response to our prayers.

Second, you'll learn the *priority* of prayer in ministry. Four times in John 17 Jesus said that God the Father "sent" Him into the world (vv. 3, 18, 21, 25). On two occasions Jesus said He was one with the Father (vv. 11, 21). And in verses 1 and 5 He asked His Father to glorify Him with the glory He had with Him before the world began.

Now, if I were to say to you, "I was sent from the Father," you'd probably reply, "Ummm—what did you just say?" I would respond, "Yeah, you heard me! I was sent from the Father; He sent me down here. And there's more: I'm one with the Father. And you know what else? I had glory with the Father before the world began." Any mere human being who claimed oneness with the Father, who claimed to have been sent by the Father, who claimed to have glory with the Father, would be carted off, put in a room, and the door would be slammed shut, locked, and the key thrown away. Those kind of folks aren't allowed to roam free in our world. *But this is exactly what Jesus said.* Why did He say such things? Because what He said was true. Jesus Christ is God. The Gospel of John was written to prove that Jesus is divine.

> *Lord, let me be reminded of the importance of keeping my mind stayed on You. I know that I think of You more than I did before cancer entered my life. I know that I have become more sensitive to Your will and to being holy than ever before. I am reminded of the verse from Micah that I wrote in my journal yesterday. That is what I want to be in my life to honor You and live for You and to serve You with my whole heart. Help me to know that in these days when my heart could be troubled as I think about the uncertain future, that "Thou wilt keep him in perfect peace whose mind is stayed upon Thee."*

So here's the key question: If Jesus Christ is God, then why does He have to pray? And here's the answer: When He walked upon this earth,

Jesus voluntarily agreed to live in dependence upon the Father as an example of how we are to live. So if Jesus Christ, with all His power and perfection, made prayer a priority in His life, then where ought prayer to fit in your life and in mine?

AN ANCHOR FOR THE SOUL

During his last illness, the great Reformer John Knox asked that certain Bible passages be read to him every day. Every day his wife read aloud a chapter out of Ephesians, the stirring words of Isaiah 53, and the great prayer of John 17.

Early on the morning of November 24, 1572, Knox asked his wife to read 1 Corinthians 15, known as the resurrection chapter. When she finished, he said, "That's a right comfortable chapter." And he was correct. When you're getting ready to die, you want to read about the resurrection.

Four hours later, just before he died, Knox called his wife to his bedside and said, "Honey, read to me that chapter where I first cast my anchor." John 17 is the text she read. Early in his ministry Knox had cast his anchor at John 17, and the priorities he found there guided him through his enormously productive life. When he was about to meet his Maker, he wanted to hear one last time about the anchor which had given him stability, direction, and hope.

I pray that God would enable you and me to cast our own anchor in John 17. It is there that we will be enabled to focus on the precious priorities of our Savior. And it is there that we will find the strength to carry out those priorities. There's a reason it's called "the greatest prayer ever prayed." But we'll only discover that reason when we adopt its agenda as our own.

Chapter Twelve

SECRETS OF THE DIRECTED LIFE

Have you ever gone through a period when you felt as if you were losing control?

Can you point to a time when the riptides of life randomly pushed you this way and that, robbing you of your sense of purpose?

Have the incessant pressures, daily hassles, and mounting responsibilities of living ever conspired to eat away at that essential, inner-feeling of direction you so desperately needed?

When Jesus uttered the prayer recorded in John 17, He gave to us the secret of His own inner-directed life. His plan offers an alternative to being buffeted mercilessly by the powerful cross-currents of life. If we follow His plan, we may correct the sense of inner-lostness that affects some of us all of the time and all of us some of the time.

A LIFE-TESTED PRAYER

Jesus not only offered this prayer to His Father, He *lived* by it. He gloriously perfected it in His own practice. He was and is uniquely the best expositor of His own remarkable prayer.

Remember when this prayer was uttered! He was just about to step out of the light of ministry and friendship and simple human pleasures into a horror of darkness. After this very night—in just a few short hours—everything would change. The bright days of His ministry were almost gone. A

Night like no other awaited around the corner—a tidal wave of darkness, a sea of pain, an utter isolation that could not be measured.

And just before He stepped into this deepest of trials, He lifted up His eyes and prayed to His Father in the hearing of His men. This prayer was born out of the crucible of Christ's life and comes from a heart of mingled emotions. Here the Chief Shepherd is about to embrace the cross and leave His sheep behind. On His heart weighs an infinite pressure; in His soul rules an internal passion. This petition burning within must get out in prayer. In some ways, it is an extremely intimate and private moment. And yet in His love and grace, He uncovers His heart and allows us to listen in to His words. He leaves us with this prayer as a love gift, that we may examine it, ponder it, imitate it, and begin to understand its great riches.

He gave us this prayer so that we could learn how to live better for the glory of God. He had you and me on His heart that night. He did not pray merely so that we could admire His prayer; He prayed so that its principles could transform our lives.

> *I am excited to be here and to be talking with You before I start the day! First, I want to thank You again for the great time that we shared yesterday at Lake Jennings. That place is very special to me, and I feel a wonderful sense of Your presence whenever I go there to pray and to walk. I was certainly amused by the women at the guard station who questioned me when I started into the campground. In their words, "We don't have too many people walk through here dressed in a suit and tie!" I told them I was there to get rid of some stress, and that was certainly the truth.*

A SURPRISING KEY WORD

What is the key word in John 17? The term *world* would be a good candidate; it appears many times in the text. *Glory* would work, too. Jesus uses the term time and again. But perhaps the best choice is one of the smallest words in the text.

As.

In this tiny two-letter word, I believe we may find the key to appropriating John 17 for our own benefit. In essence, the word *as* takes the prayer of Jesus to the Father and applies that prayer to us. I have underlined this word in my Bible wherever it appears in John 17. Note the many appearances of this word:

• Verse 2: "*As* Thou gavest Him authority over all mankind, that to all whom Thou hast given Him, He may give eternal life." The *as* in that verse reminds us that you and I have the same *life* in us that Christ has in Him.

• Verse 11: "And I am no more in the world; and yet they themselves are in the world, and I come to Thee. Holy Father, keep them in Thy name, the name which Thou hast given Me, that they may be one, even *as* We are." Here we learn that we have the same *security* that Christ has.

• Verse 14: "I have given them Thy word; and the world has hated them, because they are not of the world, even *as* I am not of the world." This verse teaches us that we have the same sense of *hostility from the world* that Jesus has.

• Verse 18: "*As* Thou didst send Me into the world, I also have sent them into the world." Here we see that we have the same *mission* that Jesus had when He came to this planet.

• Verse 21: "That they may all be one; even *as* Thou, Father, art in Me, and I in Thee, that they also may be in Us; that the world may believe that Thou didst send Me." We have the same *unity* that Jesus has with the Father.

• Verse 22: "And the glory which Thou hast given Me I have given to them; that they may be one, just *as* We are one." We have the same *glory* that Christ has with the Father.

• Verse 23: "I in them, and Thou in Me, that they may be perfected in unity, that the world may know that Thou didst send Me, and didst love them, even *as* Thou didst love Me." Here we are reminded we have the same *love* Christ enjoys from the Father.

Taking all of this together, we find that Jesus' relationship with the Father is the pattern for our relationship to Jesus Christ. In other words...

> *If we will be to Jesus what Jesus is to the Father,*
> *then Jesus will be to us what the Father is to Jesus.*

What a tremendous truth! This takes our Lord's prayer out of the purely "theological" realm and puts it right down where you and I live. As I see Jesus relating to His Father, I learn how He wants me to relate to Him. And I can grow in my faith on the basis of that truth.

TWO KEY PRINCIPLES

Alone among human beings, the Lord Jesus Christ, from the moment He was born, knew exactly what He was supposed to do and stayed on course every minute of His life. Not once did He veer off course. He faced all the pressures and the riptides and the cross-currents we do, but He never lost sight of His goal, nor for one moment did He step away from what God had called Him to do. As we watch His relationship to the Father, we come to understand what He expects of us as we relate to Him.

In John 17, Jesus gives to us two principles about relating to the Father. Both will immeasurably enrich our life with Christ. These are key principles of the directed life.

1. Jesus lived His life by divine purpose

When Jesus was twelve years old, He and His parents took a trip to Jerusalem. When it was time to leave, His parents lost track of Him and spent a couple of anxious days searching—until they finally located Him in the temple. They began to chide Him for His absence and He replied, "Why is it that you were looking for Me? Did you not know that I had to be in My Father's house?" (Luke 2:49). Even at this young age, Jesus knew His purpose.

On one occasion many years later, His disciples told Him that He needed to eat to replenish His strength. Jesus replied, "My food is to do the will of Him who sent Me, and to accomplish His work" (John 4:34). Just before He healed the blind man in John 9, He said, "We must work the works of Him who sent Me, as long as it is day; night is coming, when no man can work" (John 9:4).

Almost every place you turn in Jesus' life, you get the sense that here was a Man driven by a divine purpose. It was *everything* to Him—food, water, air, sunlight, rain—life itself. All of the pressures, anxieties, and hostilities that surrounded Him never got in His way. Why not? Because He had His mind fixed on the goal of doing the will of God.

The book of Hebrews gives us an idea about what was going on in His mind even before He was born: "Behold, I have come (in the roll of the book it is written of Me) to do Thy will, O God" (Hebrews 10:7). Jesus was a man fueled by divine purpose. It rang in His voice. It throbbed in His veins. It shaped His every waking hour. This, then, is the key to His directed life.

And what was that purpose? He states it succinctly in John 17:2: "Even as Thou gavest Him authority over all mankind, that to all whom Thou hast given Him, He may give eternal life." The purpose of Jesus Christ on this earth was that He might be the source of eternal life for all those who had been given Him by the Father.

Seven times in this passage Christ speaks of Christians as having been given to Him by the Father (verses 2, 6 [twice], 9, 11, 12, and 24). Someone has said that the love gift of God to the world is Christ, while the love gift of Christ to the Father is Christians.

In John 10:10 Jesus says, "I came that they might have life, and might have it abundantly." Jesus said that he came "to seek and to save that which was lost" (Luke 19:10). He said, "For even the Son of Man did not come to be served, but to serve, and to give His life a ransom for many" (Mark 10:45).

Even though we will never be called upon to become the Savior of the world, it is still true that a divine purpose must direct our lives. Our frustration and loss of inner-directedness often comes when we lose sight of our goal, when we forget the purpose for which we are here. We grow weary when we get caught up in side issues, when we chase rabbits, when we pursue tangents instead of keeping our minds fixed on the goal.

May I ask a personal question? *What is your own purpose in life?* What has God called you to do? As you look at your background and temperament and gifts and life circumstances, what do you believe is God's purpose for you? Whatever that purpose is—homemaker, teacher, postal worker, store clerk, gas station attendant, elected official, etc.—God has called you to fulfill it as a special assignment from Him.

- You're not "just" a teacher; *you are God's representative in the classroom.*
- You're not "just" an elected official; *you are God's instrument in government.*
- You're not "just" a homemaker; *you are God's servant in the family.*

This perspective changes everything. Is it possible to change diapers to the glory of God? You bet, if that's where you belong. Is it possible to deliver mail to the glory of God? Certainly, if that's where God has called you. God's purpose for you may not have anything to do with preaching or counseling or directing a radio ministry or leading a choir or any number of activities we often associate with "God's work." God's work is whatever He has called you to do. And if you know that you are fulfilling the divine purpose intended for you at this season of your life, it's much easier to resist those enticing cries that try to seduce you away from your true calling. Knowing your divine purpose gives you a stability and strength that leads to victorious living.

2. Jesus lived according to divine power

A divine power infused everything our Lord did. Jesus said He lived by divine purpose, but the power to accomplish that purpose came from the Father. Jesus accomplished His purpose only by relying on the power of God the Father.

When Jesus said to His disciples in Matthew 28:19, "Go therefore and make disciples of all the nations, baptizing them in the name of the Father and the Son and the Holy Spirit," He prefaced His command by saying, "All authority has been given to Me in heaven and on earth." In other words, He was saying to His disciples (and to us), "As the Father has empowered Me to accomplish My mission, now I, in turn, am empowering you to accomplish your mission. I have authority delegated to Me from the Father, and now I give that authority to you to accomplish the task."

The same idea was in His mind in John 17:18: "As Thou didst send Me into the world, I also have sent them into the world." He was sending His disciples out with the same power and authority that He Himself had received from the Father. Jesus knew His purpose and He carried out that purpose by the will and power of God Almighty.

In the same way, if we're to carry out the purpose God has given to us, we need a power outside ourselves. Our own strength is insufficient for carrying out what God has called us to do.

> *Lord, I see the principle again in Your Word that seclusion away from the masses and the pressures of the people is absolutely necessary if we are to have anything to say to or give to the people. I am struggling this very day with this whole issue of seclusion and separation. When I read today the words of the disciples, "Everybody's looking for you," I felt that I understood to some degree what that felt like. Certainly not the whole world is looking for me nor are they looking for me for the same reasons that they looked for You, but the principle is the same. Lord, You are the Son of God, and You took the discipline and determination to get away from the crowds so that You could get alone with the Father. I pray for an increasing discipline in my life to do that very thing!*

This is where the Word of God steps away from much of the positive-thinking "truth" of today, which says, "Get a goal in your mind as Jesus had. Fix that purpose central in your thinking, steer toward that goal, and you can do it."

But it isn't true. It's a lie. Yes, I can get the purpose in mind; I can discover what God wants me to do. But if I have to depend on my own power, I fall far short! Apart from His empowering, I *can't* do it. "Without Me," Jesus reminded us, "you can do nothing" (John 15:5).

Jesus insists that the power to accomplish our purpose comes from God alone. The only way we can stay on target is by giving ourselves to His authority. How does this work? Author Jamie Buckingham illustrated it well in a column he wrote a few years ago, just before Operation Desert Storm erupted in the sands of the Middle East:

> This month marks the 200th anniversary of John Wesley's death. On February 24, 1791, six days before he died, the 88-year-old minister asked his helper to bring paper and quill to his bed.
>
> For years Wesley had followed the attempts of William Wilberforce, a member of Parliament, to have slavery abolished in England. In 1774, Wesley had written *Thoughts on Slavery*, a book that had influenced Wilberforce to push for abolition. Sadly, all attempts had been unsuccessful.
>
> Now, on his deathbed, Wesley heard that Wilberforce was about to give up the fight. The vested interests of slavery in Parliament were too powerful.
>
> With faltering hand, Wesley wrote Wilberforce a powerful letter of encouragement.
>
> "Unless God has raised you up for this very thing, you will be worn out by the opposition of men and devils. But if God be for you, who can be against you? Are all of them stronger than God?

"O be not weary of well-doing! Go on, in the name of God and in the power of His might, till even American slavery (the vilest that ever saw the sun) shall vanish away before it.

"Reading this morning a tract wrote by a poor African, I was particularly struck by the circumstance that a man who has a black skin, being wronged or outraged by a white man, can have no redress; it being a law in all our Colonies that the oath of a black man against a white goes for nothing. What villainy is this!

"That He who has guided you from youth up may continue to strengthen you in this and all things is the prayer of, dear sir, your affectionate servant. John Wesley."

Wilberforce received the letter after Wesley died. He vowed to once again take up the fight. It took 16 years, but in 1807 the British empire abolished slavery.

I'm writing this on January 16. Our nation is just hours away from a horrible war. The phone rang as I was typing this column. It was one of our church members calling to say another pastor in town—a Southern Baptist—was under fire. Some of his members disagreed with his leadership style. They didn't like the way he shook hands at the door. He wasn't "evangelistic" enough. They wanted him out and were going to bring it up at the business meeting that night.

I could hardly believe it. Here our nation is on the eve of war, and church members have started their own war, pulling their pastor away from spiritual warfare for the nation to fight for his life!

I did what Wesley did. I stopped typing, picked up the phone and called my pastor friend across town. "Remember who put you here—not man, but God. Listen to their criticism and improve, but do not flee nor allow them to chase you off. Hold your ground. You are needed here...."

As I talked, I could tell from the tone of his voice that his drooping shoulders were coming up, his eyes were brightening. Fire was returning to his bones.[1]

That's what happens when we live our lives by the power of God. As both Wilberforce and Jamie Buckingham's friend learned, if you attempt to accomplish God's purposes through your own power, "you will be worn out by the opposition of men and devils." But if you draw on the infinite might of our Heavenly Father, you will be able to say along with John Wesley, "if God be for you, who can be against you? Are all of them stronger than God?"

No, they're not. Thank God!

FIVE PROMISES TO HELP US STAY ON TRACK

As Jesus begins His prayer He says, "Father, the hour has come." Seven times in John's Gospel this phrase, "the hour has come," is used. What hour was Jesus talking about? The hour in which He would finally and ultimately accomplish His goal, the redemption of the world.

The cross was the central point in Jesus' life. He fixed his face like a flint toward the cross—that was His goal, His purpose, His mission. And whenever we read in the Scripture about "the hour," we're talking about *that* hour.

This term is first found in John 2. Jesus was attending a marriage feast at Cana of Galilee, along with His mother and His disciples. When the wedding party ran out of wine, Mary said to her Son, "They have no wine." Jesus replied, "Woman, what do I have to do with you? My hour has not yet come" (John 2:3, 4).

Jesus was not rebuking His mother nor was He refusing to deal with the lack of wine, for we know by reading the story that He went ahead and turned some water into wine. Jesus was saying to His mother, "The time for Me to be submissive to the authority of man in the hour of My crucifixion is not yet here. I will not be placed under authority to man. I will do what you ask of Me, but I want you to understand that this is not My purpose right now. My purpose is the cross and I will not let the activity even of a marriage ceremony distract Me from that purpose." The first thing you learn when you live according to the divine plan is this:

1. Nothing can distract you

Isn't that where most of us get lost along the way? We start out to accomplish our purpose, then some other good thing comes along and before we know it, we've taken a left turn, landed just a few degrees off target, and the goal gets lost. But when we keep God's purpose in mind, we are empowered by the Spirit of God to accomplish it. When we live according to a divine plan, nothing can distract us.

The second occurrence of the phrase is found in John 7:30: "They were seeking therefore to seize Him; and no man laid his hand on Him, because His hour had not yet come." The same thing is said in John 8:20: "These words He spoke in the treasury, as He taught in the temple; and no one seized Him, because His hour had not yet come." I submit that when you live according to God's plan, not only can nothing distract you, but:

2. Nothing can destroy you

Isn't that exciting? Jesus did not fear destruction because He was on target with His plan. He knew what God had prepared for Him. He knew He would one day go to the cross and that therefore nobody could destroy Him before God was done with Him. And He lived in the confidence and the courage of that understanding.

If we're not careful, we can misunderstand this truth. I remember

Dr. J. Vernon McGee talking about a man who had been studying the doctrine of predestination. The man became so entranced by the idea of God's sovereign protection that one day he made a boast to Dr. McGee.

"You know, pastor, I'm so convinced that God is keeping me, no matter what I do, that I believe I could step right out into the midst of the busiest traffic at noontime, and if my hour had not yet come, I would be perfectly safe."

"Mister," Dr. McGee replied, so very characteristically, "if you step out in traffic at high noon, your hour *has* come."

If it's so easy to get this principle out of perspective, then, what is the proper way to apply it? Allow me to give one small illustration. When I first began to preach across the country and started flying a lot, a cold fear swept over me whenever we taxied out to the runway to take off. I began to think I might never see my children or my wife again.

One day a friend gave me a statement I will never forget. I wrote it in my Bible: "Remember this, Jeremiah. God's man, living in the center of God's will, is immortal until God is through with him." I'd never thought of it like that before. If I'm living in the center of God's will, according to God's plan, He is responsible to protect me so that I might fulfill His will for my life. Jesus understood that and therefore never worried. No one could lay a hand on Him because His hour had not yet come.

The phrase next appears in John 12:27. Jesus is praying and says, "Now My soul has become troubled; and what shall I say, 'Father, save Me from this hour'? But for this purpose I came to this hour."

Here the Lord is wrestling with His own heart. The time of His struggle has come. This is a pre-Gethsemane anguish. In Gethsemane He would say, "Let this cup pass from Me, but nevertheless, not My will but Thine be done." Here in chapter 12 He's going through a time of inward suffering, a period of internal torture and grief. The Scripture tells us simply that He was "troubled." But note what Jesus says. He *doesn't* say, "What shall I *choose*?" The choice already has been made in His heart. He says, "What shall I *say*?" Even though He is troubled, He understands that for *this* hour He had been born. This tells me that when you live according to God's plan:

3. Nothing can discourage you

Jesus did not let His overwhelming sense of anguish discourage or dissuade Him from the task. He understood the importance of both His hour and His goal. And that overwhelming purpose kept Him from being discouraged and prevented Him from fleeing the plan God had laid out for Him.

The next instance of the phrase is found in John 16:32: "Behold, an hour is coming, and has already come, for you to be scattered, each to his own home, and to leave Me alone; and yet I am not alone, because the Father is with Me." Jesus understood the significance of that hour. He knew that when the hour came, He would be left alone, abandoned, rejected. All of His disciples would forsake Him. When He hung on the cross, only one lone disciple stood there with His mother. Everyone else had fled.

The same pattern is repeated today. If you have a goal and purpose in mind, you're going to discover it can get lonely. Sometimes you're the only one who understands what God wants you to do. Sometimes you feel as if nobody in the world can comprehend it but you. That was Jesus' situation. And if ever there were a time when He could have been tempted to give up His goal, it was then. He'd invested thousands of hours into the lives of His disciples, building their faith, modeling godliness, trying to help them understand His redemptive purpose—and yet they didn't understand. He prophesied accurately that they would desert Him and run away. Yet Jesus understood that when you live according to God's plan:

4. Nothing can disappoint you

Jesus realized that though His disciples might have abandoned Him, He still had the Father. As He says in this passage, "Yet I am not alone, because the Father is with Me."

The final occurrence of this phrase is found where we started, John 17:1. We learn here that when you live according to God's plan:

5. *Nothing can defeat you*

Remember that Jesus speaks these words in victory, not in defeat. He lifts His eyes to heaven and we hear Him saying, almost as if we were there, "Father, the hour has come! Glorify Thy Son!" It's not an admission of defeat but a shout of victory. *This* was the hour for which He had been living since the moment He was born in Bethlehem. He came into the world to die, and as the hour approached, His goal was in sight, His purpose before Him—and *this* was His hour of glory. This was the hour when the Son of Man would end His earthly labors; when the Lord of Glory would be made sin for our benefit; when the central prophecies of the Old Testament would be fulfilled; when the sun would refuse to shine; when death would be swallowed up in victory. This was the hour of triumph and glory for Jesus Christ. Finally it had arrived. And so He exults, "This is the hour! The goal has been reached!"

Jesus could not be defeated because He lived out a purpose from God through the power of God. He carefully followed a daily schedule that never let Him get lost along the way. And if we follow His example, we can enjoy the same kind of victory He did. Talk about adventure!

EPITAPH FOR A FAITHFUL LIFE

John 17:4 provides a mighty epitaph for the sinless life of Jesus of Nazareth. In anticipation of His finished work upon the cross, He says, "I have finished the work which You have given Me to do" (NKJV). What a tremendous thought!

Have you ever wished you could say such a thing about one *day*, let alone your whole life? Notice that Jesus did not say, "I have finished ALL the work there is to do." That's the way many of us would read it. We get so caught up in perfectionism and workaholism that we think the only way to achieve happiness is to say, "I have finished all the work there is to do." That's a trap and a hopeless cause.

One of my seminary professors, Haddon Robinson, used to tell us that the ministry was like dipping out of the ocean with a teaspoon. "You dip and dip and dip," he said, "and you look back, and it's all still there." If you think you will find joy only in being able to finish all the work there is to do, you will never find joy.

But read Jesus' statement carefully: "I have finished the work which You have given Me to do." Do you see the difference? Not all the work there is, but all the work that's mine. I can buy into that. My goal is not to find out how much work there is to do; my goal is to find out the work God has given *me* to do. Lock onto that. When at the end of his most fruitful life the apostle Paul wrote, "I have finished my course," he was merely echoing what Jesus said here. He meant that he had finished the work God had given him to do.

> In reading Your Word today, I was overwhelmed to be reminded of Hezekiah's prayer for extended life. You answered him and gave him his request! The sad thing about it is this: he did not learn his lesson. He went right back to doing his own thing . . . showing the Babylonians the treasures of the Lord. And Nebuchadnezzar came and took those treasures away along with Daniel and many of his contemporaries. Lord, help me to learn my lessons well. I don't want to have gone through all of these things and then do some stupid thing like Hezekiah did. Nonetheless, I do want to emulate what Hezekiah did as the result of his healing. He sang his songs with stringed instruments every day in the house of the Lord. Let me never forget to praise You, O Lord, for what You are doing in my life. How I love you for Who You are and for what You have done for me!

It is possible to so lock onto the goal and purpose that God has for your life that, if you are empowered by the Spirit of God and stay on schedule by a daily plan, you can come to the end of your days, look up into the face of your Father and say victoriously, "God, I have finished the work which You gave me to do."

Perhaps you have seen the slogan that says, "God put me on this earth to accomplish a specific purpose. *Right now I'm so far behind that I will never die.*" That's funny, but it misses the point. It is possible to live in such a way that you *do* accomplish God's purpose for you on this earth.

How Are You Serving Your Generation?

When I was ordained many years ago, my father preached the ordination service using this text: "David...served his own generation by the will of God" (Acts 13:36, KJV). Then he reminded me (as he has many times since) that there is only one thing God can ever ask of us: That we serve our own generation by the will of God. We are called to do the work God has given *us* to do. That's it.

I wonder, are you bold enough and courageous enough to do this? Do you have the willingness before God to find out what your work is? Do you know what God has given you to do? Have you a purpose clearly in mind? Are you willing to submit that purpose to the empowering of the Holy Spirit and then stay on schedule to see it done? God says, "Here's my plan and purpose for you."

So stay on schedule, my friend. God has a purpose fixed for you. It's a point somewhere out there in the distance. He wants you to accomplish it. He will empower you to do it. And if you stay on schedule, He will see that nothing—not distractions, not destruction, not discouragement, not disappointment, not defeat—will keep you from finishing your work. Then you, like Paul, will be able to say, "I have finished my course." Then you, like Jesus, can say, "I have finished the work You gave me to do."

Good words, those.

I doubt there are any better words in any language anywhere in the world.

Chapter Thirteen

A PERSONAL MAP
TO BURIED TREASURE

No self-respecting treasure hunter would ever set off on an adventure to dig up buried riches without a map. You know the kind of map I'm talking about—yellow with age, frayed at the edges, heavy with the odor of pirates and gun powder and massive oak treasure chests. The kind of map that hails from a wild land where adventurers of long ago used machetes to cut their way through a dense jungle, looking for just the right spot to unpack their shovels and dig into the moist earth to bury their cache of diamonds and rubies and sapphires and gold. The kind of map that features a big, black X to mark the exact spot where the treasure lies.

I assume that you'd like to find that kind of map, wouldn't you? I know I would!

Well, guess what? In a very real sense, I already have discovered such a map…*and I think I can help you find one, as well.*

The treasure map I have in mind will lead you as surely to hidden treasure as any that Long John Silver ever fingered—but I guarantee it will do you a lot more good than any map ever did him. He's long since departed this world and left his gleaming baubles behind, but the treasure you uncover through your map will last eternally.

You see, the kind of treasure map I'm thinking of is one you draw yourself, based on the riches you find through answered prayer. I'm talking about a treasure map that has no one but you for its author.

HELP FOR THE JOURNEY

When we concluded the last chapter, I am sure we all agreed that staying on schedule should be a high priority. But if you're like me, you know how tough that can be! Life gets so hectic; we get caught up in the journey and forget where we are going. Once in awhile we have moments of awareness and realize we are not where we want to be. How do we keep from getting so far off track?

I have made a personal discovery that I think will help, an effective way to measure spiritual progress and hold myself accountable to God's schedule for my life. The secret? Several months ago I began to keep a spiritual journal.

I first encountered journaling about half a century ago when my uncle Clifford came to live with us for awhile. Clifford was a quiet man who had faced a great many challenges in his life. But he was a godly saint and years before he came to live with us, he began keeping a diary. I can still remember him dragging out his seven-year journal after dinner and asking us if we knew what had happened on a particular date in any of the previous seven years. No doubt most of us kids yawned as we humored our uncle by listening to him read his short diary entries.

I remember thinking it seemed strange that someone would take the time to write down what happened each day and then refer to it later. What was the point? My uncle went to be with the Lord this year and I regret that I never had the opportunity to tell him of my new love for journaling.

My personal interest in keeping a journal began several years ago when I first read Gordon MacDonald's book, *Ordering Your Private World*. Gordon began keeping a journal twenty years before he wrote his book and for him it started this way:

I became impressed by the fact that many, many godly men and women down through the centuries had…kept journals, and I began to wonder if they had not put their fingers upon an aid to spiritual growth. To satisfy my curiosity, I decided to experiment, and began keeping one for myself.[1]

While I did not start journaling right away, I did begin to wonder what it would be like to cultivate such a habit. A few years later I read something Bill Hybels wrote that lodged in my heart. He talked about journaling as a way to slow down the RPMs in his life:

> I have a high energy level in the morning. I can't wait to get to the office to start the day's work. And once the adrenaline starts flowing, the phone starts ringing, the people start coming, I can easily stay at ten thousand [RPMs] until I crash at night. So I decided to start journaling…. The amazing thing is what happens to my RPMs when I write. By the time I've finished a long paragraph recapping yesterday, my mind is off my responsibilities. I'm tuned in to what I'm doing and thinking, and my motor is slowed halfway down.[2]

What Bill described about his life matched my own experience exactly. I often struggled with taking the time at the beginning of the day to focus on and listen to God. All I could think of was the huge list of "to do's" that awaited me. Could Bill be right about the power of journaling to slow one down at the beginning of the day?

Then in 1994, while recovering from surgery, I received a copy of Gordon MacDonald's book, *The Life God Blesses*. Since I was confined to a recliner for a few days, I started to read his book…and could not put it down. As long as I could remember, I had always wanted God to bless my life. My bout with cancer had taken my desire to a whole new level.

Once again, Gordon talked about his personal discipline of journaling. This time he mentioned that he journaled on his computer. For some odd reason, that clicked with me. That very day I began to keep a record of God's dealings with me, using my computer. Since that time I have been keeping a daily journal. When I say "daily," I do not mean that I never miss a day. But I have become so committed to this discipline that whenever I do miss a day, I don't let it rob me of the joy of returning as soon as possible. More than anything else, this practice has reminded me that my walk with God is a daily experience that can be chronicled and measured.

A GREAT ASSET

Keeping a journal can become a great asset to those who embark upon the adventure of prayer. For me, as well as for most others I know, the quest to know God and to learn how to communicate with Him more effectively has been more of a journey than an event. Journaling not only provides a road map for where I've been, it often reminds me of where I'm heading.

The Christian life was never meant to be static, but dynamic! As Paul wrote, "Even though our outward man is perishing, yet the inward man is being renewed day by day" (2 Corinthians 4:16, NKJV). The apostle saw spiritual growth as a process that requires personal discipline. That's what he meant in 1 Timothy 4:7 when he encouraged Timothy to discipline himself for godliness' sake. In *The Life God Blesses*, Gordon MacDonald defines discipline like this:

> Discipline is that act of inducing pain and stress in one's life in order to grow into greater toughness, capacity, endurance, or strength. So spiritual discipline is that effort pressing the soul into greater effort so that it will enlarge its capacity to hear God speak and, as a result, to generate inner force (spiritual energy) that will guide and empower one's mind and outer life.[3]

In this book I have attempted to place the practice of prayer within the framework of personal discipline. While I have described it as an adventure, I have not tried to make it sound like a lazy adventure or an easy excercise. I have been discovering over these past months that many of the spiritual disciplines are interdependent. In my case, the spiritual discipline of journaling has helped me in the spiritual discipline of prayer.

WHAT IS A JOURNAL?

Journals have existed throughout all ages of history. In a sense, large sections of the Bible itself could qualify as journals. The book of Job is written in the style of a journal, telling the story of one man's suffering and his encounter with his "comforting" friends. Ecclesiastes is another kind of journal which records Solomon's attempt to find meaning in life apart from God. The four Gospels are written accounts of oral stories which circulated for years about the life of Christ. In a way they are the journals of the early church. The Book of Acts is a journal that records how the church grew under the leadership of Peter and Paul and the early disciples.

More recent church history would have huge gaps were it not for the journals of men like St. Augustine, David Livingstone, David Brainerd, Blaise Pascal, Soren Kierkegaard, John Wesley, Jim Elliot, and many others. By one writer's count, there are more than *nine thousand* published journals! And we are immeasurably richer because they exist.

A journal is a diary, but it's much more than that. It is a daily account of your walk with God. It often includes a list of prayers that God has answered. Sometimes it involves interaction with Scripture. It can become one of the best methods for charting your spiritual growth. Someone has defined a journal like this:

A journal is a book in which you keep a personal record of events in your life, of your different relationships, of your responses to things, of your feelings about things—of your search to find out who you are and what the meaning of your life might be. It is a book in which you carry out the greatest of life's adventures—the discovery of yourself.[4]

As helpful as this is, I like Donald Whitney's definition better because he sees journaling from a distinctly Christian perspective:

A journal…is a book in which a person writes down various things. As a Christian, your journal is a place to record the works and ways of God in your life. Your journal also can include an account of daily events, a diary of personal relationships, a notebook of insights into Scripture, and a list of prayer requests. It is where spontaneous devotional thoughts or lengthy theological musings can be preserved. A journal is one of the best places for charting your progress in the other Spiritual Disciplines and for holding yourself accountable to your goals.[5]

WHY KEEP A JOURNAL?

There are benefits in keeping a personal journal. Let me suggest just five:

1. To help you remember what God is doing in your life

The Bible is filled with instructions to make "remembering" a high priority. Consider these:

Remember His marvelous works which He has done, His wonders, and the judgments of His mouth (1 Chronicles 16:12, NKJV).

Remember now your Creator in the days of your youth, before the difficult days come, and the years draw near when you say, "I have no pleasure in them" (Ecclesiastes 12:1, NKJV).

But recall the former days in which, after you were illumi-
nated, you endured a great struggle with sufferings (Hebrews
10:32, NKJV).

Remember therefore from where you have fallen; repent and
do the first works, or else I will come to you quickly and remove
your lampstand from its place—unless you repent (Revelation
2:5, NKJV).

We all have occasions when we cannot see what God is doing in our
lives. Our faith may be weak, our eyes dimmed by sickness or discouragement. But there is no missing what God has done in the past. If a
record is kept of God's dealings with us, we will be encouraged to keep
trusting Him in difficult times. I think Asaph had this in mind when he
penned the words of this Psalm: "I will remember the works of the Lord;
Surely I will remember Your wonders of old. I will also meditate on all
Your work, and talk of Your deeds" (Psalm 77:11–12, NKJV).

> *The most awesome answer to prayer came on the day that the test
> results from the second surgery were announced. I will never forget that
> moment of exhilaration in our living room. We knew and know now
> that this was not a final answer to our prayer for complete healing, but
> it was a wonderful milestone along the way. I knew that day that You
> had done that for us . . . for me in answer to not only our prayers, but
> the prayers of so many others as well.*

Writing down what you ask God to do, and then recording His
answers, will spur you on to greater faith and trust in Him. Use it as your
own map to hidden spiritual treasure!

2. To help you respond to life honestly

We often have a rosier appraisal of our walk with God than it may war-
rant. We tend to color our record in bright shades when a more subdued

hue is called for. Yet we can't grow until we get brutally honest about where we truly are. If we believe we are growing when we are not, we will never get started with God. Keeping a journal forces us to respond to life honestly. Ronald Klug, who has written one of the few books on spiritual journaling, notes:

> Writing in a journal can…help us to be more honest with ourselves. One friend told me, "Writing in my journal helps me be truthful. If I write something false about my life, I can't get by with it. My rationalizing stands out when I see it in black and white."[6]

Gordon MacDonald also discovered that writing in his journal made it easier for him to face the truth about himself:

> Slowly I began to realize that the journal was helping me come to grips with an enormous part of my inner person that I had never been fully honest about. No longer could fears and struggles remain inside without definition. They were surfaced and confronted. And I became aware, little by little, that God's Holy Spirit was directing many of the thoughts and insights as I wrote. On paper, the Lord and I were carrying on a personal communion. He was helping me, in the words of David, to "search my heart."[7]

When we read the book of Psalms, we see how honestly David dealt with life. Sometimes we are shocked by the bluntness of his words. How do you respond when he cries out, "How long, O Lord? Will You forget me forever? How long will You hide Your face from me? How long shall I take counsel in my soul, having sorrow in my heart daily. How long will my enemy be exalted over me?" (Psalm 13:1–2, NKJV)

Two months before missionary Jim Elliot was killed by the Auca Indians, he made this honest entry into his journal:

In studying Spanish, I left off English Bible reading and my devotional reading pattern was broken. I have never restored it. Translation and preparation for daily Bible lessons is not sufficient to empower my soul. Prayer as a single man was difficult, I remember, because my mind always reverted to Betty. Now it's too hard to get out of bed in the morning. I've made resolutions on this score before now but not followed them up. Tomorrow it is to be—dressed by 6:00 A.M. and study in the Epistles before breakfast. So help me God.[8]

Journaling can help you to be honest in your growth in faith. And honesty is the required first step in anyone's spiritual walk.

3. To help you reflect on the meaning of your experiences

When I checked out of the Mayo Clinic a couple of years ago, my Christian doctor sat me down and gave me a little speech. It went something like this: "David, I've never had cancer, but I've dealt with so many people who had it that I almost feel as if I've had it myself. I want to tell you something that I think you will find to be true in the days ahead. You will never, *ever* again drive by the ocean and see just the ocean."

Call the man a prophet! All of a sudden, my perception of life was enhanced from grainy black and white to high resolution Technicolor. I began to see and notice things that I had never before stopped to notice. Everyday experiences were no longer lost in the shuffle of schedules and appointments. I began to observe a pattern in what God was doing in my life.

And when did my more acute observations begin? When I started to write down what was happening to me and when I took the time to reflect on them afterwards. I think this is what Arthur Gordon had in mind when he wrote the following words in *A Touch of Wonder*:

> How do we keep in the forefront of our minds the simple fact that we live in an indescribably wonderful world? It's not easy. Routine dulls the eye and the ear. Repetition and familiarity fog the capacity for astonishment. Even so, moments come to all of us when everything suddenly seems fresh and new and marvelous. The gift of awareness makes possible some of our happiest hours. We need to be receptive to it and grateful for it.[9]

Journaling enables us to better appreciate the world around us, as well as God's hand on our life. It's hard to miss a big, black X marking the treasure when you're staring straight at it!

4. To help you record the progress of your spiritual journey

In his book *First Things First*, Steven Covey makes this interesting statement about journals:

> Keeping a personal journal empowers you to see and improve, on a day-by-day basis, the way you're developing and using your endowments. Because writing truly imprints the brain, it also helps you remember and apply the things you're trying to do. In addition...as you take occasion...to read over your experiences of past weeks, months, or years, you gain invaluable insight into repeating patterns and themes in your life.[10]

While Covey was looking at this process from a management or business perspective, his comments are transferable to the spiritual realm. It's really true that "the unexamined life is not worth living." When we don't keep track of our progress, we will never be motivated to grow as we might. This is especially true of prayer. When we begin to take the time (as I am learning to do) to write out some of our prayers, we discover areas of weakness that need to be strengthened and patterns of sin or foolishness that need to be corrected. We can also discover good patterns that are worth strengthening and encouraging.

> *I love the promise that though I eat the bread of adversity and drink the water of affliction, the Lord will not hide His teachers from me. They will be there to say to me, "this is the way, walk in it." Truly there seems to be a greater sense of the importance of Your leading in my life because of the affliction and adversity. I also sense, Lord, that in quietness and in confidence I will find new strength. I am sensing a quiet and deep working in my life during this time!*

One of the hidden benefits of computer journaling is the exact way my word processor records dates and times. In the program I use, the date and time of each entry is entered into the text of the journal at the top of the page. I also click in the time at the end of each day's entry. It is amazing what this little routine has done for my consistency. When I look over my journal at the end of the month or at the end of the year, I can see the missing dates. I have discovered from this review that certain situations make me especially vulnerable to missing my time with the Lord. Knowing what those situations are, I can prepare counter strategies to help me overcome my lapses. Without journaling, I'd still be in the dark. But my map to hidden spiritual treasure has shown me the glint of gold!

5. To help you regain lost momentum

One of the women in our church made an appointment to see me some time ago. As we began our time together she said, "Pastor, I love the Lord with all my heart; I know I'm a Christian. I've walked with God for as long as I can remember. But something is wrong and I do not know what it is! I've got the spiritual blahs. I don't know how to explain it. There are days when I don't want to read the Bible and I don't want to pray. Sometimes I don't even want to come to church."

With tears in her eyes and anguish in her voice she pleaded, "Pastor Jeremiah, what is wrong with me?"

After encouraging her and praying with her, I gave her an assignment. "I want you to go to the stationery store and buy a notebook," I said. "Each day I want you to write in that notebook. Begin by putting the date at the top of the page. After you have read your Bible, ask God to give you something from your reading that you will want to write down. Write down the things you are praying for and the way you feel about your walk with God. Do that every day for the next thirty days. Then each day go back and read what you wrote the day before. Follow that pattern for the next thirty days, then come back and tell me what God has done in your life."

When she returned one month later, I didn't have to ask if things were better. As soon as she stepped into my office I could tell something had changed. Her face beamed with the joy of the Lord. She told me that about two weeks into the process, she began to see what had happened. God met her in a fresh, new way and the relationship was restored.

Gordon MacDonald made this same discovery. He found journaling to be a valuable resource in regaining lost spiritual momentum:

On those days when coldness has been more than a matter of outer New England temperatures, I have found myself unable to produce hardly a coherent word from soul-level. The journal has helped at such times.... I have learned to write and describe to the Father in journal form my hardness of soul and spirit. Usually after three or more paragraphs of frank talk, I find the inner stone begins to break up.[11]

Every Christian will experience dry times. If there is no mechanism in place to bring about restoration and renewal, the devil will use those dry times to torment us. Journaling is a good way to prevent it.

WHAT SHOULD I WRITE IN MY JOURNAL?

There is no right or wrong way to do a journal, but there are several areas you might want to concentrate on. First, write about your *experiences*. Write about the people you meet, the things you accomplish, the problems you encounter, your impressions about the way your life is going. I have discovered that by writing out the things that are making my heart heavy, my load seems lighter and I am able to progress to the more productive parts of my spiritual journey.

Second, I recommend that you write out your *prayers*. Some may find this difficult to do; I admit that when I first started it, I felt as if I were praying to my computer. But I soon got past that and began to realize the benefit of being precise in my conversation with the Lord. This may not be for everyone, but for those who have a difficult time staying on track as they pray, this can be a great help. Once again, Bill Hybels gave me some insight. He wrote, "A good way to learn to pray specifically is to write out your prayers and then read them to God. Many people find they are better able to concentrate if they put pen to paper and arrange their assorted thoughts into an organized format. I've been doing this for several years, and I find that it helps me in several ways. It forces me to be specific; broad generalities don't look good on paper. It keeps my mind from wandering. And it helps me see when God answers prayers."[12]

> *Oh God, let me not forget You. Let this record that I am keeping be a reminder to me each day that You are the Rock of my Stronghold and without You I am a 0 (zero). I have so often tried to prove myself and have gone at it all alone leaving You out. I have learned*

and am learning that there is no real victory or joy in the Christian life unless there is total dependence upon God. I pray, dear Lord, that You will never let me become a heap of ruins. Oh God, spare me from the day of grief and desperate sorrow. I want to finish strong and make a greater impact for You than I have ever dreamed of. Please hear this prayer from Your servant, David Jeremiah!

Third, it's extremely helpful to write down the *insights you get from God's Word.* Since I began to journal, I have been reading five chapters from Scripture each day and asking God to cause His truth to intersect with my life in such a way that I am impacted that very day. For many of us who spend long hours studying the Bible so that we can teach it to others, finding a way to let the Word of God touch us personally and devotionally can be a real challenge. I have found that this simple plan of reading and responding to the Bible has helped me greatly. After I finish my reading, I enter into my journal the verses God has used to encourage or confront me. Often I write down the thoughts those verses have produced in my heart.

Fourth, I find it useful to write down *quotes from books I am reading.* Several years ago I began the practice of reading a chapter from a book on prayer each day. I usually did this just before I prayed and I found it to be a source of great motivation and encouragement. It became a positive part of my daily discipline. In fact, many of the quotes on prayer scattered throughout this book were taken from my journals. These thoughts have greatly enriched my walk with God. I sometimes feel so blessed to be surrounded by some of the greatest men and women of God who have ever lived. Through their books they have become like personal friends.

Fifth, I would encourage you to write about your *doubts and fears.* Morton Kelsey in *The Other Side of Silence* describes how he expresses emotion in his journal:

I...write about my angers and fears and hurts, depressions and disappointments and anxieties, my joys and thanksgivings.... In short, I set down the feelings and events that have mattered to me, high moments and low.... The journal is like a little island of solid rock on which we can stand and see the waves and storms for what they really are.[13]

Gordon MacDonald also sees the benefits of recording our emotions:

A key contribution of the journal became its record of not only the good moments, but the bad times as well. When there came times of discouragement, even of despair, I was able to describe my feelings and tell how God's spirit ultimately ministered to me to strengthen my resolve. These became special passages to look back upon; they helped me celebrate the power of God in the midst of my own weakness.[14]

When I examine the entries in my journal during the days of my illness, I see many fearful prayers. Here is an entry I made on the day before I was to have surgery:

Lord, we are being stretched in our faith, and I know that is for a good purpose. Please help us to continue to trust You with each day and with each bit of news that we receive. As I have already prayed, dear Lord protect Donna's heart on Monday. Keep her in the center of Your will...in Your hands and wrap Your arms around her in a very special way. May those who come to stay with her be an encouragement to her and a blessing! Lord I know that my times are in Your hands.... You are able to do above and beyond all that I can even ask or think. I trust You even when I am afraid!

When we record our fears and anxious moments, later we can see how great a God we have, a Warrior who can conquer our fears and slay those anxieties! But there is also great benefit in the moment of writing. Somehow, in getting those fears out into the open, their power over us diminishes. This has been not only my experience, but that of many others as well. Why not make it your own?

LEARNING FROM YOUR JOURNAL

While there is great benefit in journal writing, the greatest advantage comes from harvesting its contents. I had never connected the term "harvesting" with the practice of journaling until I read Ronald Klug's book, *How To Keep A Spiritual Journal.* In the closing chapter of his book he talks about the value of going back at certain intervals and rereading larger sections of our journals. This can be done at the end of a month or at the midpoint of the year or even at the end of each year.

Before I read about harvesting I had never completely read through my journals. At the end of this past year, I decided to read my journals through as a way of preparing myself for the new year. I decided to index them by names, subjects, and Scripture references. I was not far into the process before I realized I had waited far too long to undertake this process. (As I write this chapter, I still am not finished with my indexing project. My experience suggests that it's best not to wait longer than six months before you begin to harvest your journal.)

As I reread my journals, I began to be impressed with some significant thoughts:

• There were certain periods in my life when journaling was very difficult for me. These were so predictable (as I looked back on them) that I could have entered the dates in my calendar before they occurred.

• I was consistently asking God for some things that I needed to take responsibility for myself. I was surprised how often I asked Him for the same thing. There was nothing wrong with my persistence, but I could almost hear God saying to me as I read these entries, "David, why don't you just get control of your life and deal with these issues?"

• I was brought to tears on more than one occasion as I read my prayers in an early entry, then the record of God's answer in a later entry. God really heard me! He really did answer my prayer!

• I saw that I had a lot of growing to do in the art of intercession. I've made a good start, but I have a long way to go.

I could list many other insights I gained from harvesting my journal, but these illustrate the point. Luci Shaw sums up the benefits of journal harvesting with these words:

> Rereading a journal is like viewing a forest from a helicopter. From that fluid height you can see the larger contours of the land, the way the trees clump and break, the vivid color contrasts between evergreens and maples, the cliffs and streams and rocks that interrupt the flow of the landscape. When you are lost in the forests of daily crisis, caught in the underbrush, you cannot know where you are. Only from the height of passing months and years can you see your life in proportion and with true perspective.[15]

MAKE YOUR OWN MAP!

I cannot begin to describe how enormously the practice of journaling has strengthened my spiritual walk and deepened my prayer life. Often it has served as a lifeline in very stormy seas. It does not surprise me that someone as brilliant as Jonathan Edwards would pen these words in his journal shortly after his conversion: "I seemed often to see so much light exhibited by every sentence, and such a refreshing food communicated, that I could not get along in reading, often dwelling long on one sentence to see the wonders contained in it, and yet almost every sentence seemed to be full of wonders."[16]

And Edwards's testimony is far from unique! Earlier I quoted Luci Shaw, widow of the late Christian publisher, Harold Shaw. While these days she is a faithful guide to journaling, it was not always so:

> All my life long I've thought I should keep a journal. But I never did until a few years ago, when the discovery that my husband, Harold, had cancer suddenly plunged us into the middle of an intense learning experience, facing things we'd never faced before. Confronted with agonizing decisions, we would cry out to the Lord, "Where are you in the middle of this?" It suddenly occurred to me that unless I made a record of what was going on, I would forget. The events, details, and people of those painful days could easily become a blur. So I started to write it all down.[17]

Even C. H. Spurgeon, celebrated as the "prince of preachers" in the last half of the 1800s, said, "I have sometimes said when I have become the prey of doubting thoughts, 'Well now, I dare not doubt whether there be a God, for I can look back in my Diary, and say, On such a day, in the depths of trouble, I bent my knee to God, and ever I had risen from my knees, the answer was given me.'"[18]

Is it any wonder that so many of the people we consider spiritual giants were devoted to the practice of journaling? I don't think so. I think we would do well to consider the question posed by one astute observer of great Christian saints. He asks, "How did men like Edwards and Whitefield become so unusually conformed to the image of Christ?" He answers, "Part of their secret was their use of the Spiritual Discipline of journaling to maintain self-accountability for their spiritual goals and priorities. Before we give all the reasons why we cannot be the kind of disciples they were, let us try doing what they did."[19]

I think that's outstanding advice. We could use a few more like Edwards and Whitefield. If journaling could help nurture men and women like them, then by all means, let's start journaling.

I'm convinced that believers like them could create some pretty spectacular spiritual treasure maps. And you know what? I believe God just might be calling you to be one of those map makers.

RECOMMENDED READING

Arthur, Kay. *Lord, Teach Me To Pray In 28 Days*. Eugene, OR: Harvest House Publishers, 1982.

Boice, James Montgomery. *The Sermon On The Mount-An Exposition*. Grand Rapids, MI: Zondervan Publishing House, 1972.

Bounds, E.M., compiled by Leonard Ravenhill. *A Treasury Of Prayer*. Minneapolis, MN: Bethany Fellowship, Inc., 1961.

Chambers, Oswald, edited by Harry Verploegh. *Prayer: A Holy Occupation*. Grand Rapids, MI: Discover House Publishers, 1992.

Cymbala, Jim. *Fresh Wind, Fresh Fire*. Grand Rapids, MI: Zondervan Publishing House, 1997.

Eastman, Dick. *The Hour That Changes The World*. Grand Rapids, MI: Baker Book House, 1978.

Hallesby, O. *Prayer*. Minneapolis, MN: Augsburg Publishing House, 1931, 1959.

Hybels, Bill. *Too Busy Not To Pray*. Downers Grove, IL: InterVarsity Press, 1988.

Keller, W. Phillip. *A Layman Looks At The Lord's Prayer*. Chicago, IL: Moody Press, 1976.

Lockyer, Dr. Herbert. *The Power Of Prayer*. Nashville, TN: Thomas Nelson Publishers, 1982.

MacArthur, John. *Jesus' Pattern Of Prayer*. Chicago, IL: Moody Press, 1981.

Moody, D.L. *Prevailing Prayer*. Chicago, IL: Moody Press, n.d.

Packer, J. I. *I Want To Be A Christian*. Wheaton, IL: Tyndale House Publishers, 1977. (Contains a major section on the Lord's Prayer.)

Sanders, J. Oswald. *Prayer Power Unlimited*. Chicago, IL: Moody Press, 1977.

Stedman, Ray C. *Jesus Teaches On Prayer*. Waco, TX: Word Books, 1975.

Taylor, Jack R. *Prayer: Life's Limitless Reach*. Nashville, TN: Broadman Press, 1977.

Tirabassi, Becky. *Let Prayer Change Your Life*. Nashville, TN: Thomas Nelson Publishers, 1990, 1992.

Torrey, R.A. *The Power Of Prayer And The Prayer Of Power*. Grand Rapids, MI: Zondervan Publishing House, 1924.

Wiersbe, Warren W. *Listen! Jesus Is Praying*. Wheaton, IL: Tyndale House Publishers, Inc., 1982.

NOTES

INTRODUCTION

1. Andrew Murray, *With Christ in the School of Prayer* (Old Tappan, NJ: Spire Books, 1975), 5.

2. Ibid., 6.

3. Jim Cymbala, *Fresh Wind, Fresh Fire* (Grand Rapids, MI: Zondervan Publishing House, 1997), 29.

4. Ibid., 49.

5. Jack Taylor, *Prayer: Life's Limitless Reach* (Nashville, TN: Broadman Press, 1977), 22.

6. John Piper, *Desiring God, Tenth Anniversary Expanded Edition* (Sisters, OR: Multnomah Publishers, Inc., 1996), 146.

7. Ibid., 146, 147.

8. Oswald Chambers, *Prayer-A Holy Occupation* (Grand Rapids, MI: Discovery House, 1992), 7.

9. Eugene Peterson, *The Message* (Colorado Springs, CO: NavPress, 1994).

10. Murray, 2.

11. Piper, 139.

12. Chambers, 130

13. Murray, vi.

14. Chambers, 33.

15. Murray, 26.

16. Ibid., 3.

17. Bill Hybels, *Too Busy Not To Pray* (Downers Grove, IL: InterVarsity Press, 1988).

18. Trisha Rhodes, *The Soul at Rest* (Minneapolis, MN: Bethany House, 1996), 16.

CHAPTER ONE

1. Andrew Murray, *With Christ in the School of Prayer* (Old Tappan, NJ: Spire Books, 1975), 33.

2. J. Oswald Sanders, *Effective Prayer* (Chicago: Moody Press, 1969), 19.

3. Oswald Chambers, *Prayer-A Holy Occupation* (Grand Rapids, MI: Discovery House, 1992), 101.

4. James Montgomery Boice, *Romans – Volume 1: Justification by Faith, Romans 1–4* (Grand Rapids, MI: Baker Books, 1991), 89.

5. Andrew Murray, *With Christ in the School of Prayer* (Springdale, PA: Whitaker House, 1981), 5–6.

6. Bill Hybels, *Too Busy Not to Pray* (Downers Grove, IL: InterVarsity Press, 1988), 74.

CHAPTER TWO

1. Donald S. Whitney, *Spiritual Disciplines for the Christian Life* (Colorado Springs, CO: NavPress, 1991), 226.

2. Ibid., 3.

3. John Piper, *Desiring God Tenth Anniversary Expanded Edition* (Sisters, OR: Multnomah Publishers, Inc., 1996), 152.

4. Bill Hybels, Too Busy Not to Pray (Downers Grove, IL: InterVarsity Press, 1988), 11.

5. Piper, 156

6. Quoted by Whitney, *Spiritual Disciplines,* 237.

7. Oswald Chambers, *Prayer-A Holy Occupation* (Grand Rapids, MI: Discovery House, 1992), 97.

CHAPTER THREE

1. Ron Mehl, *Surprise Endings* (Sisters, OR: Multnomah Publishers, Inc., 1993), 139–141.

2. Bill Hybels, *Too Busy Not to Pray* (Downers Grove, IL: InterVarsity Press, 1988), 9.

3. Ibid., 13.

4. Oswald Chambers, *Prayer-A Holy Occupation* (Grand Rapids, MI: Discovery House, 1992), 120.

5. George Mueller, quoted in Donald Whitney, *Spiritual Disciplines for the Christian Life* (Colorado Springs, CO: NavPress, 1991), 77.

6. Chambers, 111.

7. Ibid., 25.

8. From a photocopy of an unnamed source.

9. Ibid.

CHAPTER FOUR

1. James Montgomery Boice, *The Sermon on the Mount* (Grand Rapids, MI: Zondervan Publishing House, 1972), 183–4.

2. Donald S. Whitney, quoting Andrew Murray in *Spiritual Disciplines for the Christian Life* (Colorado Springs, CO: NavPress, 1991), 66.

3. Trisha Rhodes, *The Soul at Rest* (Minneapolis, MN: Bethany House, 1996), 26, 27, 28.

4. Andrew Murray as quoted in *Christianity Today*, February 5, 1990, 38.

5. Oswald Chambers, *My Utmost for His Highest* (Grand Rapids, MI: Discovery House).

6. Evelyn Christenson, *A Journey Into Prayer* (Wheaton, IL: Victor Books, 1995), 24.

7. Andrew Murray, *With Christ in the School of Prayer* (New York: Fleming H. Revell Company, n.d.).

8. Boice, 186.

CHAPTER FIVE

1. Dr. Ross Campbell, "How to Really Love Your Child," *Worldwide Challenge*, May/June 1989, 27.

2. John Piper, *The Pleasures of God* (Portland, OR: Multnomah Press, 1991), 93, 94.

3. John MacArthur, *Jesus' Pattern Of Prayer* (Chicago, IL: Moody Press, 1981), 46.

4. Donald W. McCullough, *The Trivialization of God* (Colorado Springs, CO: Navpress, 1995), 103–4.

5. Ibid., 113.

6. Martin Luther, as quoted in MacArthur, 49.

7. McCullough, 112.

8. From an oral presentation given by Brennan Manning.

CHAPTER SIX

1. Ann Landers, "Big fish in a small pond? You're doing swimmingly," *The Oregonian,* May 18, 1991, C14.

2. Andrew Murray, *With Christ in the School of Prayer* (New York: Fleming H. Revell Company, n.d.), 27.

3. Clarence Edward Macartney, *Macartney's Illustrations* (New York: Abingdon Press, 1946), 409.

4. Evelyn Christenson, *A Journey Into Prayer* (Wheaton, IL: Victor Books, 1995), 19.

5. Ron Lee Davis, church newsletter, First Presbyterian Church of Fresno, California, n.d.

6. Oswald Chambers, *Prayer-A Holy Occupation* (Grand Rapids, MI: Discovery House, 1992), 143.

7. Ibid., 136.

8. Murray, 28.

9. Macartney, 72.

10. Story included in an InterVarsity Christian Fellowship mailing.

11. Bill Hybels, *Too Busy Not To Pray* (Downers Grove, IL: InterVarsity Press, 1988), 71.

12. Henry Blackaby and Claude V. King, *Experiencing God* (Nashville, TN: Broadman & Holman Publishers, 1994), 23.

13. Ibid., 23.

14. Ibid., 122.

15. Ann Landers, "Class of '73: There're Beamers and smiling beamers," *The Oregonian,* September 26, 1991.

16. Blackaby and King, 19.

CHAPTER SEVEN

1. Ray C. Stedman, *Jesus Teaches on Prayer* (Waco, TX: Word Books, Publisher, 1975), 72.

2. Michael Horton, "Our Father In Heaven," *Modern Reformation*, 3.

3. Jim Bakker with Ken Abraham, *I Was Wrong* (Nashville, TN: Thomas Nelson Publishers, 1996), 531–3, 541.

4. John Piper, *Desiring God, Tenth Anniversary Expanded Edition* (Sisters, OR: Multnomah Publishers, Inc., 1996), 168, 169.

5. Ibid., 172, 173.

6. Oswald Chambers, *Prayer-A Holy Occupation* (Grand Rapids, MI: Discovery House, 1992), 108.

7. Anonymous

8. George Mueller, quoted in Donald Whitney, *Spiritual Disciples for the Christian Life* (Colorado Springs, CO: NavPress, 1991), 77.

CHAPTER EIGHT

1. Simon Wiesenthal, *The Sunflower,* quoted in Lewis B. Smedes, *Forgive & Forget* (New York: Pocket Books Simon & Schuster Inc., 1984), 162–3.

2. Ibid., 165–6.

3. Ibid., 160.

4. Ibid., 189–90.

5. John MacArthur, *Jesus' Pattern of Prayer* (Chicago, IL: Moody Press, 1981), 131.

6. Smedes, 18.

7. Mike MacIntosh, *The Tender Touch of God* (Eugene, OR: Harvest House, 1996), 173.

8. Ibid., 174.

9. Quoted by J. I. Packer, *I Want To Be A Christian* (Wheaton, IL: Tyndale House Publishers, Inc., 1977), 214–5.

10. Philip Yancey, *The Jesus I Never Knew* (Grand Rapids, MI: Zondervan Publishing House, 1995), 204.

CHAPTER NINE

1. Paul Thigpen, "Lead Us Not Into Temptation but Deliver Us From Evil," *Discipleship Journal,* Issue sixty-two, March/April, 1991, Volume 11, Number 2, 39.

2. These "Benefits of Temptation" are adapted from Thigpen.

3. D.A. Carson, "Matthew" in *The Expositor's Bible Commentary,* Volume 8 (Grand Rapids, MI.: Zondervan Publishing House, 1984), 173.

4. The Anglican Prayer Book for Epiphany IV quoted in J. I. Packer, *I Want To Be A Christian* (Wheaton, IL: Tyndale House Publishers, Inc., 1977), 222.

CHAPTER TEN

1. R. Kent Hughes, *Disciplines of a Godly Man* (Wheaton, IL: Crossway Books, Good News Publishers, 1991), 107–8.

2. Ibid., 108.

3. Quoted in David Robinson, "Is Anyone In Charge?" *Command,* Fall 1992, Vol. 41, No. 3, 7.

4. A. M. Overton, "He Maketh No Mistake," Croft M. Pentz, compiler, *Speaker's Treasury of 400 Quotable Poems* (Grand Rapids, MI: Zondervan Publishing House, 1963), 73.

5. Dave and Jan Dravecky, *Do Not Lose Heart* (Grand Rapids, MI:

Zondervan Publishing House, 1997), Section V, introductory paragraph.

6. R. Laird Harris, Gleason L. Archer, Jr., Bruce K. Waltke, *Theological Wordbook of the Old Testament* (Chicago, IL: Moody Press, 1980), 427.

7. Source unknown.

8. M. W. Gass quoted in John MacArthur, Jr., *Jesus' Pattern of Prayer* (Chicago, IL: Moody Press, 1981), 66.

9. Larry Lea, *Could You Not Tarry One Hour?* (Lake Mary, FL: Creation House, Strang Communications Company, 1987), 180.

CHAPTER ELEVEN

1. James Patterson and Peter Kim, quoted in "God plays small role in U.S. morality," *The Oregonian,* August 7, 1991.

2. Woodie W. White, *Good News,* January/February 1986.

CHAPTER TWELVE

1. Jamie Buckingham, "The Power of Encouragement," *Ministries Today,* March/April 1991, 4.

CHAPTER THIRTEEN

1. Gordon MacDonald, *Ordering Your Private World* (Chicago, IL: Moody Press, 1984), 141.

2. Bill Hybels, *Too Busy Not To Pray* (Downers Grove, IL: InterVarsity Press, 1988), 103–104.

3. Gordon MacDonald, *The Life God Blesses* (Nashville,TN: Thomas Nelson Publishers, 1994), 41.

4. Harry J. Cargas and Roger J. Radley, *Keeping a Spiritual Journal* (Garden City, NY: Doubleday, 1981), 8.

5. Donald S. Whitney, *Spiritual Disciplines For The Christian Life* (Colorado Springs, CO: NavPress, 1991), 195.

6. Ronald Klug, *How To Keep A Spiritual Journal* (Minneapolis, MN: Augsburg Press, 1993), 19.

7. Gordon MacDonald, *Ordering Your Private World,* 141.

8. Elisabeth Elliot, ed., *The Journals of Jim Elliot* (Old Tappan, NJ: Fleming H. Revell, 1978), 58.

9. Arthur Gordon, *A Touch of Wonder* (Old Tappan, NJ: Fleming H. Revell, 1974), 165, quoted by Ronald Klug, *How To Keep A Spiritual Journal* (Minneapolis, MN: Augsburg Press, 1993), 23.

10. Steven Covey, *First Things First* (New York: Simon & Schuster), 64–65.

11. MacDonald, 202.

12. Hybels, 47.

13. Morton Kelsey, *The Other Side Of Silence,* quoted by Luci Shaw in *Life Path* (Portland, OR: Multnomah Press, 1991), 32.

14. MacDonald, 142.

15. Luci Shaw, *Life Path–Personal and Spiritual Growth through Journal Writing* (Portland, OR: Multnomah Press, 1991), 34.

16. Ibid., 51.

17. Ibid., 201.

18. Ibid., 201.

19. Ibid., 205.

Scripture Index

Genesis 17:5 177
    20 38
    32:22–32 39
    50:20 156
1 Samuel 12:23 38
1 Chronicles 16:12 228
Psalm 7:1–2 165
    13:1–2 230
    16:8 95
    19:14 94
    22:3 172–73
    22:19–21 165–66
    24:7 174
    25:19–21 166
    32:6 39
    33:18–19 167
    34:4 167
    50:15 162
    77:11–12 229
    91 61
    91:14–15 162
    104 120–21
    104:2 181
    107:9 122
    119:11 164
    138:1–2 96
    145:5 180
Ecclesiastes 12:1 228
Isaiah 2:4 104
    4:2 180
    6 45
    11:8 104

53 205
56:7 39
57:15 182
Daniel 3:17–18 163–64
4:34–35 174
4:37 174
Micah 4:3 104
Habakkuk 1:5 133
Matthew 2:2 174
4:1 156
4:4 . . . . .120, 122
5:10–12 . . . . .160, 165
5:21–26 145
6:5 77–79
6:7–8 79–80
6:9–13 . . . . .71–77, 124–26, 131–32, 184–88
6:14–15 139
6:33 105
7:7–11 20–32
9:38 41
10:23 . . . . .160, 165
18:19–20 43
18:21–35 139–43
19:25–26 177
23:34 163
24:6 160
24:7 122
24:20 . . . . .160, 165
26:41 41
28:19 213
Mark 1 36–38
2:17 13
10:45 211–12
11:23–24 41
Luke 2:49 210–11

3:11 130
6:5 126
6:20–21 122
7:47 150
9:58 130
11:5–8 51–62
12:29 130
12:33 130
15:12 128
17:21 103
18:1–8 52–62
18:13 41
19:8 130
19:10 211
22:32 41
22:44 56
John 1:4 181
1:49 174
2:3–4 216–17
4:34 211
5:40 54
6:35 120
7:30 217
8:20 217
9:4 211
10:10 211
11:26 162
12:26 115
12:27 218–19
15:5 . . . . .55, 214
16:32 219
16:33 163
17 . . . . .190–96, 202–5, 207–8
17:1–5 196–97
17:1 220

17:2 . . . . .209, 211

17:4 220

17:6–19 197–99

17:11 209

17:13 194

17:14 209

17:18 . . . . .209, 213

17:20–26 199–202

17:21 209

17:22 209

17:23 209

18:36 40

Acts 1 42

2:41 42

2:43,47 42

4:24–31 42

6:4 42

6:5–6 42

12:5 42

12:12 42

13:3 42

13:36 222

14:23 42

17:25 122

Romans 1–4 150

4:19 177

4:20–22 177

4:25 162

8:20–22 121

8:34 195

13:14 164

1 Corinthians 9:25 40

10:12 161

15 205

15:20–28 175–76

2 Corinthians 4:16 226
Galatians 4:4–7 85
Ephesians 3:20–21 179
Philippians 4:13 55
Colossians 1:17 123
    1:29 40
    2:1 39
    4:2 39
    4:12 39
2 Thessalonians 3:1–2 . . . . .70, 165
1 Timothy 1:17 174
    2:2 160
    4:7 . . . . .159, 226
    6:6,8 127
    6:12 40
    6:15 174
    6:15–16 181
2 Timothy 2:22 164
    3:12 165
    4:16 169
    4:17–18 168–69
Hebrews 1:1–3 . . . . .94, 123
    4:16 64
    5:7 55
    7:25 195
    9:24 195
    10:7 211
    10:19–22 87
    10:32 229
    11:37 162–63
    13:8 183
James 1:5 41
    1:12–15 154–56
    4:2 70
    4:3 132

    4:7 . . . . .41, 164
    4:8 . . . . .164, 172
    5:13–15 41
    5:16–20 41
1 John 1:5 181
    3:1 85
Jude 20 41
Revelation 1:5 174
    2:5 229
    3:21 105
    15:3 174
    21:23 182
    22:20 38

Topical Index

Abraham, ...38, 157, 177
Armstrong, Herbert W., ...178
Asaph, ...229
Augustine, ...63, 227
Bakker, Jim, ...127–29
Barley, Henry, ...111
Baxter, Richard, ...106
Boice, James Montgomery, ...27
Bonaparte, Nappoleon, ...174
Bonar, Andrew, ...12, 25–26, 27
Brainerd, David, ...227
Bryant, David, ...43
Buckingham, Jamie, ...214, 216
Burnham, Dave, ...45
Busy lives, ...35, 45–46, 48, 96–97
Calvin, John, ...90, 192
Calvinism and Arminianism, ...70–71
Campbell, Ross, ...83
Cancer, author's experience with, ...11, 13, 33, 96, 120, 123,
. . . . .167–68, 204, 229, 231–32
Carson, D. A., ...160
Chambers, Oswald, ...48, 56, 58, 59, 78, 110, 132, 139
Cho, Pastor, ...186
Church unity, ...199–201
Covey, Steven, ...232
Cymbala, Jim, ...12
Daniel, ...161
David, .162, 164, 165, 167, 222, 230
Deborah, ...162
Deliverance, ...161–64
DeNure, Dick, ...73
Dependence on God, ...12, 53–55, 94–95, 119–120

Discouragement and prayer, ...51–53, 64–65, 76, 219

Early Church and prayer, ...41–43

Edman, Raymond, ...97

Edwards, Jonathan, ...192, 239

Elijah, ...162

Elliot, Jim, ...227, 231

Esther, ...161

Evangelism, ...201–2

Faith, ...53–55, 61–62, 126

Five–finger praying, ...132–33

Fleming, Jean, ...48

Forgiveness, ...135–52

God the Father, ...85, 87, 120–21, 121–22

God: His attributes, ...90–91, 92–94, 95, 174–84

God: His will, ...107–10, 113–17, 195–96, 218–19, 220–22

Gordon, Arthur J., ...171, 232

Graafschap, Jane, ...137–38

Guilt about prayer, ...20, 233–35

Hackett, Buddy, ...146

Health and wealth gospel, ...127–31

Hendricks, Howard, ...24, 64, 203

Herbert, Lord, ...145

Hezekiah, ...221

High Priestly prayer of Jesus, ...191–205

History of prayer, ...43–45

Holy Spirit, ...25–26, 42, 193, 222, 230

Hybels, Bill, ...30, 40, 54, 126, 225, 235

Imperatives of prayer, ...21–24

Influence of prayer, ...25–27

Intercession, ...111–13, 131–33, 148, 193–95

Isaac, ...157

Isaiah, ...182

Jacob, ...39

James, ...70

January, Spencer, ...59–61

Jesus, ...103–10, 193–94, 210–16, 220–22

Jesus, His attributes, ...94, 172, 183

Jesus, instructions on prayer, ...71–75

Job, ...157, 159, 227

John, ...85

Joseph, ...156

Journaling, ...223–41

Kelsey, Morton, ...236

Kennedy, John F., ...89

Kierkegaard, Søren, ...92, 227

Klug, Ronald, ...230, 238

Knox, John, ...205

Landers, Ann, ...101, 116–17

Lauphier, Jeremiah, ...44

Lewis, C. S., ...180, 199

Livingstone, David, ...227

Lord's Prayer, ...71–75, 184–88

Luther, Martin, ...48, 94, 192

MacDonald, Gordon, ...224, 225–26, 230, 234, 237

MacIntosh, Mike, ...147

Manning, Brennan, ...98

Martha, ...162

Mary, mother of Jesus, ...216

McCullough, Donald, ...90

McGavran, Donald, ...201

McGee, J. Vernon, ...218

Mehl, Ron, ...49

Melancthon, Philip, ... : 192

Moody, Dwight L., ...111, 124

Morgan, G. Campbell, ...78

Mueller, George, .57, 113, 133–34

Murray, Andrew, ...11, 38, 75, 76, 79, 96, 105

Nebuchadnezzar, ...163, 174

Niebuhr, Reinhold, ...146

Parker, Joseph, ...55

Pascal, Blaise, ...227
Paul, ...70, 85, 159, 162, 165, 168–69, 175, 177,
. . . . .179, 181, 196, 221, 226
Pavarotti, Luciano, ...90
Persistence in prayer, ...32, 56–57, 64, 178–79
Peter, ...42, 139
Peterson, Eugene, ...145
Piper, John, ...39, 129–31
Power from God, ...212–16
Praise, ...90–98, 172–77, 186–88, 221
Prayer laps, ...186
Protection, ...217–18
Purpose in life, ...210–12, 217
Rahab, ...162
Relationship with God, ...74–75
Revival, ...43–45, 81
Robinson, Haddon, ...221
Ryle, J. C., ...191
Samuel, ...38
Sanders, J. Oswald, ...26
Satan, ...63–64, 97, 106, 156–57, 161, 166, 168, 175
Shaw, Luci, ...239–40
Simms, Roger, ...49
Simon the Pharisee, ...150
Small groups, ...45–48, 78
Smedes, Lewis, ...135–37, 137–38, 141, 146, 147
Solomon, ...227
South Korea, ...46–47
Specific prayer, ...31–32, 58–59, 167, 235
Spiritual warfare, ...97, 105
Spurgeon, Charles, .111, 192, 240
Stanley, Charles, ...151
Taylor, Jack, ...12
Tertullian, ...154
Timothy, ...159

Torrey, Reuben, ...79
Trials and temptations, ...153–61
Triple–cord prayer, ...46–48
Unanswered prayer, ...26–27, 49–51, 59–61
Von Zinzendorf, Ludwig Count Nicholas, ...43
Wesley, John, ...70, 214, 215, 227
White, Woodie, ...202
Whitefield, George, ...70
Whitney, Donald, ...36, 228
Wiesenthal, Simon, ...135–37
Wilberforce, William, ...214, 216
Wrestling in prayer, ...39–40, 55–56
Yancey, Philip, ...151